New designs for Europe

Katinka Barysch, Steven Everts, Heather Grabbe, Charles Grant, Ben Hall, Daniel Keohane and Alasdair Murray

With an introduction by the Rt Hon Peter Hain MP

ABOUT THE AUTHORS

Katinka Barysch is chief economist at the CER. **Steven Everts** is senior fellow, transatlantic relations, at the CER. **Heather Grabbe** is research director at the CER. **Charles Grant** is director of the CER. **Peter Hain** is Minister of State at the Foreign and Commonwealth Office, with responsibility for Europe, and is also the British government's representative in the Convention on the future of Europe. **Ben Hall** is former research director of the CER and now writes for the Financial Times. **Daniel Keohane** is research fellow, security and defence policy, at the CER. **Alasdair Murray** is director of the business and social policy unit at the CER.

ACKNOWLEDGEMENTS

The authors would like to thank the many people who have helped them with this volume, including Giuliano Amato, Pascale Andréani, Pervenche Berès MEP, Philip Budden, Anthony Cary, Jérôme Creel, Robert Cooper, Richard Corbett MEP, Judy Dempsey, Martin Donnelly, Tom Drew, Jean Pisani-Ferry, Jean-Paul Fitoussi, Cristina Gallach, Friedrich Heinemann, Christoph Heusgen, Catherine Hoye, Roger Liddle, Jo Leinen MEP, Kate Meakins, Julian Priestley, Catherine Royal, Leonardo Schiavo, Philippe de Schoutheete, Reinhard Silberberg, Adam Townsend and Philip Whyte.

Contents

Abbreviations

CAP	Common Agricultural Policy
CFSP	Common Foreign and Security Policy
COSAC	Conference of the Community and European Affairs Committees of Parliaments of the EU
DG	directorate-general
ECB	European Central Bank
ECHR	European Convention for the Protection of Human Rights and Fundamental Freedoms
ECJ	European Court of Justice
Ecofin	Council of finance ministers
ESDP	European Security and Defence Policy
GAC	General Affairs Council
GAERC	General Affairs and External Relations Council
GDP	gross domestic product
IGC	inter-governmental conference
IMF	International Monetary Fund
JHA	Justice and Home Affairs
MEP	Member of the European Parliament
NATO	North Atlantic Treaty Organisation
QMV	qualified majority voting
SIS	Schengen Information System

Foreword

Europe is in a phase of institution-building. The imminence of enlargement has finally forced Europe's governments to accept that the EU and its institutions need new designs. Like the workmen in Pieter Bruegel's Tower of Babel, the delegates to the Convention – government representatives plus national and European parliamentarians, from Central as well as Western Europe – are setting about their task with some determination. Let us hope that the conclusion of their labours is better-crafted than the biblical tower.

This is not a book about the Convention on the future of Europe. Many fine think-tanks have published detailed analyses of that august body's work, and will continue to do so. The essays in this volume say rather little about several issues that are central to the Convention's work, such as the 'catalogue of competences'. However, this is a book about rebuilding the EU's institutions. The authors offer a wide range of designs, some of which are very pertinent to the work of the Convention, and to the revision of the treaties that will follow it.

What these essays have in common is a non-ideological, non-dogmatic approach to the EU. The authors are more interested in what works than in political theory. They try to steer a safe course between the Scylla of fervent federalist idealism, and the Charybdis of cynical 'inter-governmental' power-politics. The underlying attitude towards the EU is one of constructive criticism.

Some of our designs are intended for the EU institutions themselves: I write on the European Council and the Council of Ministers, Ben Hall on the Commission, Alasdair Murray on the Parliament, and Katinka Barysch on the European Central Bank (we do not cover the Court of Justice in this volume). But other essays are thematic and policy-focused: myself on the question of leadership, Steven Everts on foreign policy, Daniel Keohane on defence policy, Alasdair Murray on economic reform, and Heather Grabbe on Justice and Home Affairs. We are grateful to Peter Hain for writing the introduction, in which he makes the case for a European constitution.

Charles Grant

Introduction: time for an EU constitution
The Rt Hon Peter Hain MP

The EU is not simple. The founding fathers set out to devise a political and economic order for a highly developed, culturally diverse region of the world. They wanted to create a dynamic framework – unique among international organisations – that would not just operate at the lowest common denominator of agreement. It has been remarkably successful: Europe's peace and prosperity have been assured by the founding fathers' vision of bringing us together to achieve common goals. But the corollary of dynamism is popular consent. And the risk of projects as ambitious and complex as this one is that people feel they are in a fast-moving car, without any influence over the controls.

Fifty years on, the founders' goals remain essential and viable. But around them, the needs and expectations of our citizens have developed. One of the paradoxes of the modern world is that globalisation, and increased economic interdependence, have made us all think harder about our identity and our roots. We see ourselves as, say, Geordies or Brummies, as English or Welsh, as British and increasingly as European. We have no problem carrying those different identities in our heads, and we are proud of them all. Integration and co-operation across borders have undoubtedly improved our lives in many ways. But they have not convinced us that we want to be the same. They have made many of us value our diversity, and our local and regional heritage, even more. And we want to see that reflected in our political arrangements.

We are also more demanding consumers than we were 50 years ago. And that extends to our politics, too. We want to know who is responsible for what. At the most basic level, we must know who to complain to when we see something we do not like. And we want to be able to have our say, to influence the decisions that matter to us. We want laws to address real problems, rather than make our lives more difficult, or those of bureaucrats easier.

So it is no longer good enough to hide behind the fact that, because of its unique, dynamic nature, the Union is bound to be complex. We must make it less opaque to its citizens. And the greater the number of areas in which we decide that it is best to act together, the more important it becomes for our citizens to understand how the EU works and how it safeguards their democratic rights as citizens.

The EU's complexity and uniqueness will not make this goal easy to attain. Some of the European Union's achievements are clear: war between members of the EU is all but unthinkable. The EU has created tens of thousands of jobs while preserving a system of social protection and minimum standards. But somehow it is incapable of that most basic of tasks – explaining what it is, what it is for, and who does what. This does not just affect the person in the street. None of us working in and with the EU could answer those questions without pausing to reflect. And even then, we would probably disagree with each other. Perhaps this degree of ambiguity has proved useful at times, to keep us all on board. But now this ambiguity has become an obstacle. Our citizens are turned off the EU by what seems an almost wilful complexity.

It would be complacent to think that the issue is just one of simplification. Many people feel there is something undemocratic about the EU. In my view, that feeling comes not from concerns that the Commission is unelected, or even because voter turnout for European Parliament elections is so distressingly low. It comes from a sense that there is a lack of consent to EU laws and actions.

In any political system it is important that people have a basic understanding of how it works. The more transparent the better. It would be unrealistic to argue that it is vital for all voters to understand exactly how legislation is devised, passed and implemented. But it does matter that people know who has what power and roughly what the limits of that power are. Then they can vote in local council elections on the basis of who they want to organise local services. And they use a general election to express their views on foreign policy or on how the economy should be run. In this way, governments have a claim to consent.

The problem people have with Europe is that they think they know what the EU is allowed to do, and then they discover that the goalposts have been moved, seemingly without their consent. Unless we tackle this problem, I fear we will continue to see signs of growing unease about the European project. And it will become harder to tackle the complex challenges we now face, such as making Europe a force for good in the world, or agreeing a policy on migration, even though there is public support for 'more Europe' in these areas.

Tackling this systemic problem needs more than a reordering of some articles in the treaty, or a readjusting of the institutional order. We need the courage to think again. We do not have to start with a clean sheet of paper. But we should show that we have heard the message from our citizens.

For those reasons I think we must seize the historic opportunities offered by both the Convention on the future of Europe, and the forthcoming enlargement to 25 or more countries. I personally support the ambition of Valéry Giscard d'Estaing that the Convention, on which I am the UK government representative, should aim to devise a new constitutional treaty. People are surprised to hear a British minister support this view. They think that the UK should naturally be opposed to a written constitution, because we do not have one ourselves. But as British Foreign

Secretary Jack Straw has said, what matters is what a constitution says. Opponents of any EU constitutional text want to spread fear about what it would entail. To do so is dishonest. We should be able to have a mature debate, based on the facts.

The existence of a constitution would not in itself turn the EU into a super-state. It would not inevitably increase the powers of the EU. Nor need it change the principle that those powers come from the member-states, and that anything not explicitly within the competence of the EU is reserved for the member-states. Nor would a constitution mean harmonisation, or the end of diversity and tradition.

Perhaps the fears arise because we are in new territory. We are devising a unique structure. We are not recreating the Philadelphia Convention of 1787. Perhaps it takes too much of a leap of faith to think of a constitutional order without assuming that it necessarily entails more powers for the centre. But I find it difficult to understand why so many people assume that a constitutional text for the EU means the end of the nation-states. The evidence suggests the opposite. One of the great revelations of the EU is that nation-states do not, and will not, wither away just because we choose to integrate some of our actions to mutual advantage. Nation-states remain the building blocks of the Union – and a key source of democratic legitimacy, along with a directly elected European Parliament.

A constitutional text could set out and describe the European identity, and our shared values and aims. It could clarify that diversity is one of the great strengths of the Union, thereby helping to remove the concerns many people feel about the EU threatening their traditions and way of life. It could better explain how a collective Union works for us all. A constitution could clarify how the European Union will seek to achieve its objectives; how it will deliver on the things that matter to Europe's people; how it will be organised; what the limits of its powers will be, how they will be assigned, and how we can all change things.

A constitution need not be a threat. We do not have to choose between nation-states and the European Union. We can, and do, have both. We can have the security and prosperity that comes from membership of the Union, and the traditions and way of life that belong to us. I believe the Convention on the future of Europe is right to work towards a constitutional text that reflects that reality.

★

1 New leadership for Europe
Charles Grant

★ The heads of government should propose the name of a senior politician to become chairman of the European Council. A European Congress, consisting of an equal number of MEPs and national parliamentarians, should vote 'yes' or 'no' to the choice of chairman. The chairman would represent the EU externally at the highest levels; internally, he or she would help to ensure that governments respected the decisions taken at summits.

★ The European Congress should propose the name of the president of the European Commission. The European Council would have the right to veto that choice.

★ The chairman of the European Council, the Commission president and the High Representative for foreign policy should present their annual work programmes to the Congress, which would vote 'yes' or 'no' to each of them.

★ The EU's three 'pillars' should merge, so that the EU becomes a single legal entity. This would make the Union a little less complicated and hard to understand. It would also enable the EU to adopt a constitution. This change need not and should not lead to a significant enhancement of the role of the European Commission, Court of Justice and Parliament in most areas of EU decision-making.

Who leads the European Union? Of the many fundamental questions that the Convention on the future of Europe is struggling with, this is one of the biggest, and there is currently no clear answer. That is alarming, for the EU faces an increasing number of very difficult challenges. The accession of ten new members, probably in 2004, makes it essential for the EU to reform its institutions, as well as its policies for agriculture and regional aid. The so-called Lisbon process, intended to promote economic reform and improve Europe's meagre rate of economic growth, has had, at best, a patchy record of success. The Stability and Growth Pact, which is supposed to ensure fiscal prudence in the eurozone, has been discredited by the failure of several governments to respect its rules, and needs revising. Meanwhile the successive challenges to Europe's Common Foreign and Security Policy (CFSP) in the year since September 11th – combating international terrorism, defeating the Taleban, promoting peace between Israel and Palestine, and dealing with Iraq – have highlighted its weaknesses.

This is a charged and fraught agenda for Europe's leaders. As anyone who works in a ministry, a business or an NGO knows very well, organisations cannot cope with major challenges unless they have effective leadership. This requires individuals or groups of people to think strategically, confront problems head-on, propose solutions that may entail risks, and persuade others to accept the need for change.

However, managing the European Union is, at the best of times, a particularly difficult task, for its decision-making structures do not resemble the pyramidal organisations of a nation-state or a large business. In the EU, various supranational institutions share power with the member-states: the lines of authority are mostly horizontal rather than pyramidal. No one institution is clearly in charge and able to give orders to the rest of the organisation. Nothing happens unless a broad coalition of institutions and governments agrees that it should – which is why decision-making is so slow.

So who could or should give effective leadership to the EU? The member-state holding the EU presidency, which rotates every six months? The European Commission? The European Council? Or, on a more informal basis, some sub-group of the most important countries, such as the Franco-German alliance?

In the late 1980s and early 1990s, the answers were much clearer than they are today. The Commission, under President Jacques Delors, provided real leadership. It set the agenda, promoting the plans for a single market and a single currency. It had a big influence on the treaty changes that allowed those projects to be fulfilled: the Single European Act of 1985 and the Maastricht treaty of 1991.

Working closely with the Commission, the Franco-German alliance gave the Union a solid backbone. Many of the Commission's plans only came to fruition once Chancellor Kohl and President Mitterrand had got together and endorsed them. When France and Germany agreed on a joint initiative, the other countries usually followed.

But these days the Commission is a pale shadow of its former self, while the Franco-German tandem – although twitching rather than stone-cold dead – appears to be sapped of all strength. During the four years of Jacques Santer's presidency and the past three years of Romano Prodi's, the Commission has failed to regain the pivotal position it enjoyed in the Delors era. In the growth areas of EU activity, notably CFSP, Justice and Home Affairs, and economic policy co-ordination, 'inter-governmental' methods rather than EU institutions have dominated. The Commission has not helped its own cause by seeking to play a major role in the CFSP, an area where many EU governments wish to limit its role, yet spurning the chance to take the lead in the Lisbon process of economic reform (see Chapter 4).

The Franco-German alliance has ceased to be – as it was often called – the 'motor' of European integration. Since Mitterrand stepped down in 1995 there has not been a significant Franco-German initiative. Britain and France jointly put together the scheme for a European Security and Defence Policy (ESDP), in 1998, while Britain, Spain and Portugal took the lead in pushing the member-states to accept the Lisbon agenda for economic reform in 2000.

The reasons for the decline of this alliance are partly personal: Chancellor Schröder did not get on with either Prime Minister Jospin or President Chirac, and they all made domestic affairs their priority. But the structural reasons are more important: a united Germany sees itself at the centre of the new, enlarging European Union. It is more willing to assert its own interests and – more than half a century after World War II – less prepared to carry out France's bidding because of guilt about the past. Meanwhile France is insecure about the way the Union is developing, with the imminent arrival of Eastern European states, the decline of the French language inside the EU, an increasingly dominant Anglo-Saxon economic philosophy – and a more self-confident Germany.

In many areas of EU business, the institution of the rotating presidency is supposed to provide leadership. Every six months a different member-state takes on the job of chairing EU meetings and representing the Union externally. But this institution has fallen into growing disrepute. Countries outside the Union complain about the lack of continuity in its external representation: both people and priorities change twice a year. Each new presidency pushes its own pet projects to the top of the agenda. Small countries holding the presidency, such as Belgium, which had the job in the months after September 11th, often lack the resources or credibility to speak for Europe. However, some large countries have tended to use the position as an opportunity to pursue their national interests in a sometimes shameless manner.

The arrival of Javier Solana – the High Representative for the CFSP since 1999 – and his successful diplomacy in the Balkans have highlighted the advantages of permanence in external representation. In 2000 the Centre for European Reform published

EU 2010: an optimistic vision of the future, a book about the future of Europe's institutions, which called for – among many other things – the abolition of the rotating presidency. When the book appeared, not a single EU government wanted to scrap the rotating presidency. Now a majority does. This moribund institution is certainly not the answer to Europe's lack of leadership.

But what of the European Council, the regular meetings of the heads of government and the Commission president? The European Council is supposed to allow Europe's leaders to discuss strategy and priorities in an informal setting. Some of these summit meetings have proved decisive: the Maastricht summit of 1991 laid down the plan for the creation of the euro, while that at Copenhagen in 1993 set the criteria for the Union's enlargement into Eastern Europe. The Tampere summit in 1999 agreed on a long-term agenda for closer co-operation on Justice and Home Affairs, while the Lisbon summit six months later approved plans for a ten-year programme of economic reform.

However, the European Council often fails to fulfil its original, strategic purpose, as Chapter 3 explains. With huge numbers of officials crowding around the prime ministers, the agenda has become cluttered up with very detailed and technical questions that various councils of ministers have failed to resolve. There is no longer much scope for personal intimacy or strategic thinking. Nor is there an effective mechanism for following through the declarations of the European Council: there were plenty of fine words at the Tampere and Lisbon summits, but the heads of government have so far failed to carry out many of the promises they made at those events. In any case, the arrival of ten more heads of government in 2004 will make it even harder for the European Council to work as an effective body.

Therefore the Convention needs to engage in a fundamental re-think on how the EU is led. What follows is a proposal to reshape Europe's institutions, according to six basic principles:

★ The institutions should become more effective – meaning that they have to be able to take decisions more speedily; that there should be more continuity, so that EU institutions build up permanent expertise; and that there should be better mechanisms for implementing decisions.

★ To do their job properly, EU institutions need more legitimacy. There are many sources of legitimacy, but one that needs to be tapped is that conferred on parliamentarians – whether national or European – by election.

★ At present national MPs tend to be ignorant of, and therefore hostile to, the EU institutions, partly because they have no role to play in them. Similarly, those working in EU institutions tend to be cut off from national political systems. National parliaments should therefore become involved in the institutional workings of the EU.

★ The structures of the institutions should be simplified, so that people can more easily understand how they work. The existence of three separate 'pillars' – sets of legal arrangements for decision-making – makes the EU very hard to understand.[1]

★ It is important to preserve the balance between the institutions dominated by governments, that is, the European Council and the Council of Ministers; and the 'Community' institutions, meaning the Commission, European Parliament, European Court of Justice and European Central Bank. Far too much energy and ink is wasted on theological battles between inter-governmentalists and

[1] *The first pillar, covering the business of the European Community, is concerned with policies where the EU's institutions have 'competence', such as the single market, trade, competition policy, regional and structural funds, enlargement, and asylum and visas; the Commission, Parliament and Court of Justice play an important role in most of these policies. The second pillar covers the CFSP, including the embryonic defence policy. The Council of Ministers is the lead institution. The third covers judicial and police co-operation in criminal matters, and again, the Council is in charge.*

advocates of the Community method.[2] No plan for reforming the institutions will be viable if it seeks to tilt the balance strongly in one direction or another.

★ In recent years serious rifts have emerged between the EU's smaller and larger member-states. Small states fear that large ones will try to impose some sort of *directoire* to run many EU policies without their involvement. Big states worry that small states do not understand that the CFSP will not be credible unless those with more diplomatic and military clout are allowed to take the lead. And in the co-ordination of macro-economic policy, small states worry that different standards seem to apply to them: the Council of Ministers severely reprimanded Ireland for not following EU guidelines to cut spending, but the more serious breaches of the Stability and Growth Pact by Germany, France and Italy have received kid-glove treatment. No scheme for institutional reform will succeed unless it is seen to achieve a fair balance between the interests of small and large member-states.

[2] *The 'Community method' is the type of decision-making which normally applies to the EU's first pillar: the Commission has the sole right of initiative; its proposals are debated, amended and voted upon by both the Council of Ministers (often deciding by qualified majority voting) and the European Parliament; and the European Court of Justice rules on disputes.*

A chairman for the EU

The role of the rotating presidency is likely to be abolished, or drastically reduced, at the next inter-governmental conference. But if the prime minister of the country with the presidency ceases to chair the European Council, who should take his or her place? There is a strong case for the appointment of a full-time chairman for five years (the term served by MEPs and commissioners) or for half that period. The chairman would probably have to be a former prime minister, so that he or she enjoyed the respect of his peers.

The idea of a European Council chairman or president has many supporters, including Jacques Chirac, Tony Blair, Spanish Prime

Minister José María Aznar, Italian Prime Minister Silvio Berlusconi, Valéry Giscard d'Estaing (the president of the Convention), Giuliano Amato (Giscard's deputy and a former Italian prime minister), and some of the senior officials in the Council of Ministers secretariat.

However, all those names are from large countries. It is striking that virtually no senior figure from any small member-state has expressed support for the idea. Most of the small member-states and the accession countries are strongly hostile, seeing it as a scheme to enable the large countries to override their interests. There is little chance of the smaller countries supporting this idea unless the big countries give them something substantial in return.

The tasks of such a chairman should be – as with the current presidency – to organise meetings of the European Council, set the agenda, and focus the discussion so that it tackles salient strategic issues. When disagreements among the heads of government are blocking a decision, the chairman should intervene to broker a settlement. The chairman would also become a kind of super-spokesman for the EU, explaining summit decisions to the general public.

He or she would need to remind the heads of government that they must carry out their promises. Too many pious declarations of the European Council have soon been forgotten. The prime minister of the country with the rotating presidency has lacked the time or the inclination to pick up the phone and put pressure on recalcitrant heads of government. The Commission and its president, of course, have a role to play in ensuring that summit decisions are implemented. But the Commission lacks sufficient authority to do that in the more inter-governmental areas of policy-making, such as CFSP, judicial co-operation or budgetary policy co-ordination.

A second set of tasks for the new chairman would be external. Javier Solana has given Europe a voice in foreign policy, and has achieved success in several key negotiations, such as that on the future of Macedonia and Montenegro. But he generally moves at the level of the foreign ministers. He is, indeed, the nearest thing Europe has to a foreign minister. After September 11th, Solana was in daily contact with Colin Powell, the US Secretary of State. But he did not have the clout to go and see George W Bush or Vladimir Putin. It was Prime Minister Blair, President Chirac and Chancellor Schröder who went to see Bush and Putin.

Those heads of government were right to carry out this personal diplomacy, because the EU itself lacked a leader of sufficient credibility. The Americans understood that Romano Prodi, the Commission president, could deliver neither diplomatic clout nor military force. Nor did Belgian Prime Minister Guy Verhofstadt, who then spoke for the rotating presidency, have the requisite credentials in Washington, Moscow or Beijing.

To be sure, a European Council chairman would not necessarily have sufficient standing to ensure instant access in those capitals. That would depend on the individual concerned and the influence he or she had with the EU heads of government. Other world leaders would want to speak to the European Council chairman if he or she:

★ had a track record as a successful national leader;

★ had good contacts around the world;

★ was sensitive to the national prerogatives of EU governments, as Solana has been; and

★ was also capable of expressing a common position forcefully and eloquently.

The more successful this chairman became, the less justification the leaders of big EU countries would have for their own solo diplomacy.

One criticism of the chairman proposal is that too many cooks spoil the broth. Would the chairman not be drawn into endless turf wars with the High Representative or the Commission president? To deal first with the Solana figure, not necessarily. Many prime ministers get along fine with their foreign ministers. There would be a clear delineation of responsibilities between them. The High Rep would work full time on EU foreign policy, and might spend a week or two in the Balkans or the Middle East on some negotiation. The chairman would not normally want to intrude on the High Rep's work, especially when, as is the case with Solana, the High Rep was experienced and effective. The chairman would have plenty to do in ensuring the smooth preparation of EU summits, and the speedy implementation of European Council decisions.

However, there will be occasions when the EU would benefit from a single voice at the highest level. For example, if talks between the EU and Russia on the future of Kaliningrad broke down, and Putin was on the brink of taking punitive action against Poland and Lithuania, the chairman might need to fly to Moscow to resolve the matter. Or if the US told the EU that unless European firms pulled out of Iran, it would impose new sanctions on Europe, again, the chairman would need to act.

As for potential conflicts with the Commission president, some would be inevitable. However, the way to keep such conflicts to the minimum would be to define the relationship between the European Council and the Commission very precisely, so that both figures understood their respective roles.

The Commission should be the pre-eminent authority in the areas currently covered by the first pillar. A vigorous and efficient Commission is needed to police the single market, to extend the market into new areas and to manage Community policies effectively. The Commission's frequent error – even in the period of Jacques Delors – has been to try and play a leading role in foreign policy. The larger member-states are simply not prepared to allow it such a role. If the Commission ever succeeded in winning a leading position in the Union's foreign policy, the bigger member-states would probably ignore EU institutions and co-ordinate policy among themselves. Prodi made this mistake in May 2002, when he unveiled the Commission's proposals for institutional reform. The document contained many fine ideas. Sadly, these were barely noticed: the Commission's demand for a sole right of initiative and qualified majority voting in all areas of EU foreign policy drew all the attention.

Of course, effective EU foreign policies require the involvement and support of the Commission. But that institution needs to accept a supporting role in the CFSP. It would then find that member-states became less paranoid about allowing the Commission to extend its competences in other areas, such as Justice and Home Affairs.

The European Council should set grand strategy and take the lead in foreign and defence policy. The Commission should work to implement that strategy and take charge of most internal issues, as well as external issues where the EU has competence, such as trade. Substitute *le Président* for the European Council, and *le Premier Ministre* for the Commission, and you have something like the constitutional model of the French Fifth Republic. Indeed, the relationship between France's president and prime minister perhaps offers some guidance for that between the European Council and the Commission. In France, the president and prime minister are sometimes from different political families; so could be the chairman of the European Council and the Commission president. However, France cannot provide an exact model for Europe to follow, for the French president is an authoritarian figure who gives orders. In the EU power is diffused among so many people and institutions that no one body – not even the European Council, at the apex of the system – is going to be able to boss people about.

The European Commission needs to accept that the glory days of Delors are long since gone, and that it will not set the agenda for the rest of the EU to follow. It should work within a mandate set by the European Council. But the Commission should retain its sole right of initiative for first pillar business, and have complete operational independence in the way it manages that business. Compared with the Commission of today, it should be stronger and more authoritative, but also more focused on its core responsibilities, such as business and environmental regulation, and managing the common policies.

Thus a system of twin leadership would guide the European Union. With their roles clearly defined, there should be no major structural reason for the European Council chairman to get on badly with the Commission president. Of course, some policy areas do not fall clearly into the domain of one or the other: in the co-ordination of budgetary policy, for example, or the Lisbon process of economic reform, one can imagine these two figures treading on each others' toes. But so long as the Union picks the right people for these crucial jobs, they should be able to work together, just as Solana and Chris Patten, the external relations commissioner, have managed to get along.

Bigs against smalls

A second criticism of the idea of a European Council chairman is that it would alter the balance of power between inter-governmental and Community institutions in the former's favour. Most small member-states, and most politicians of a federalist disposition, oppose the establishment of a European Council chairman for that reason.

Over the past five years or so, there has been a growing rift between large and small member-states. As it happens, all the current EU members, as well as those likely to join soon, are either large, in the sense of having around 40 million people or more; or small in the sense of having less than 17 million people. For many years the large states have been under-represented in the Council of Ministers, in terms of their votes relative to their populations. Because of the imminent arrival of ten new members, all except Poland small, the big countries have been keen to correct that anomaly. The bitter arguments at the December 2000 Nice summit were mainly about the relative voting weights of the big and the small. The 'bigs' achieved some redress, at the cost of giving up the right to having two commissioners.

During the negotiations leading up to Nice, President Chirac adopted a high-handed and sometimes downright rude manner in his dealings with leaders of small countries. This contributed to the emergence of a new spirit of solidarity among the smalls, reinforced by subsequent events. In the aftermath of September 11th the leaders of the 'big three' – Britain, France and Germany – had a private breakfast on the margins of an EU summit in Ghent. And then in November 2002 Tony Blair's attempt to hold a dinner *à trois* in Downing Street degenerated into farce when the Italian, Spanish, Dutch and Belgian prime ministers invited themselves. Smaller countries were furious that an informal *directoire* appeared to be deciding on how the EU should act in the war against terrorism.

The smalls were also suspicious of British and French plans to abolish the rotating presidency. They see that office as one which allows them – when it is their turn – to play a prominent role in the EU. And when the *Financial Times* ran a story early in 2002, saying that the British government wanted to establish an EU body on the model of the UN Security Council, with smaller states taking it in turns to sit alongside the big ones, their fears were reinforced.

After the Convention began to meet, in March 2002, it became clear that delegates from the accession countries had very similar worries to those from the smaller member-states. Even the representatives from Poland – which to most of us looks like a large country – saw the idea of a European Council president as a scheme of the large west European states to weaken the Commission, which they regard in many ways as a friend and protector.

And that is why in the spring of 2002, when British and French ministers began to promote the idea of a 'European Council president', they won no support among the smalls. This idea reinforced their fears that the bigs were trying to establish an inter-governmental leadership from which they would be excluded. The small countries drew parallels with the creation of the post of the High Representative: although Solana's job is to represent all the EU foreign ministers, in practice he talks more to those of the big three than the others, and they fear that a European Council chairman or president would similarly talk most to the big three prime ministers.

The advocates of a European Council president were not helped by some gauche diplomacy from Britain and France which, before launching the idea, made very little attempt to prepare the ground and explain the arguments. That fact in itself made the large countries look even more arrogant than usual.

In the summer of 2002, those advocates worked hard to repair the damage. British officials stressed that an EU president would mean 'more Europe', not less. If he or she flew in to see Bush in some crisis, there would be less scope for Blair or Chirac to do so. French officials suggested that there could be an informal understanding that the post should go to a politician from a small country – someone like Martti Ahtisaari, the former president of Finland, rather than a Tony Blair. Others pointed out that, after enlargement, the European Council would consists of six large countries and 19 small ones. Under any conceivable method for choosing its chairman, the views of the small members would surely prevail.

Despite these arguments, by the time of writing (October 2002), the only small country to have offered some support for the idea is Sweden. Many of the smalls worry that an EU president or chairman would introduce the kind of strong leadership that the French president, or the prime ministers of Britain, Germany, Italy and Spain exert, but which is rare among the smaller members. Many of them have coalition governments, in which the prime minister cannot take decisions except through the slow building of a consensus. The very word president, favoured by French diplomats, implies authority, pyramidal power structures and decisive leadership. The British prefer to talk of a European Council chairman, which in English sounds more collegiate. However, the word chairman translates into French as president.

One possibility might be to plump for the term secretary-general: NATO and the United Nations have secretaries-general with very few formal powers, which helps to give that title a gentle-sounding resonance. But unfortunately the Council of Ministers already has a secretary-general, in the person of Solana, who is not only High Representative but also head of the Council's administration (at some point in the future the job of secretary-general of the Council should be separated from that of the High Representative). In any case the word secretary-general would imply, to some, that the incumbent was an official, rather than a politician. And the European Council needs a figure with political authority, rather than a civil servant, to speak for it. Therefore chairman would probably be the best title. Only in Francophone countries would there be a danger of confusing him or her with the Commission president.

The European Congress

The British and French governments still hope they can persuade the smaller countries to support the idea of a European Council chairman. But they will probably fail – unless they offer some serious concessions in other areas. In particular, they will need to agree to reforms which increase the clout of the Commission and the Parliament. This is the key to winning round not only the smaller countries and accession states, but also the Germans. Chancellor Schröder has indicated that he might, if pushed, accept a European Council chairman. But he would do so only if it was clear that the creation of such a post would not shift the balance of power between the European Council

³ Le Monde,
July 23rd
2002.
and the Commission in favour of the heads of government.

One way of strengthening the legitimacy of the Commission would be to establish a European Congress, consisting of MEPs and national parliamentarians, that would meet annually. Giscard d'Estaing has floated this idea. He has written that the Congress should not have legislative powers, but that "it would be consulted on the evolution of the Union's powers and on future enlargements. It would hear an annual report from the president of the Council and the president of the Commission on the internal and external state of the Union, and it could pronounce upon, or confirm, the nominations to certain jobs."[3] The great merit of such a scheme is that it would involve national parliamentarians in the workings of the Union – not in opposition to MEPs, but working alongside them.

One role for the Congress could be to endorse – or reject – the European Council's choice of chairman. If MEPs, as well as national MPs, were given a stake in the appointment of the chairman, some of those opposed to the creation of such a post would probably withdraw their objections. A second role could be to choose the president of the Commission. A third could be to approve the Union's work programme.

On the second role, the Commission is in danger of becoming too weak to carry out its first-pillar tasks effectively. It needs to be strong enough to stand up to large countries which may, for example, oppose its rulings on illegal state aid. If the Commission president's power rested on a stronger democratic mandate than it does today, his authority and legitimacy would be strengthened. The Congress could provide that mandate.

A second argument for giving the Congress a role in the election of the Commission president is that it would make European elections more interesting, and foster the development of European political parties. Each of the main parties – the European Peoples' Party, the Party of European Socialists, the Liberals and the Greens – would go into the elections with a designated candidate for the Commission presidency. If the Congress met shortly after the elections, voters would know that they had a chance of influencing the choice of president. That might encourage more people to vote than have done in recent European elections.

The principal argument against giving the Parliament or some other assembly a role in choosing the Commission president is that it would 'politicise' the Commission. That body has a regulatory and judicial role to play, for example in prosecuting governments which do not enforce EU rules, or in approving mergers. If the election of its president led to the Commission being seen as 'left-wing' or 'right-wing', it could not easily carry out these regulatory or judicial roles in an effective manner. And its legitimacy could suffer rather than grow: all those who had voted for one party in the European elections but saw its rival 'take over' the Commission might feel hostile towards that institution.

[4] *A useful amendment to the current model would involve each national parliament voting on its government's choice of commissioner. Only a positive vote would allow the government concerned to put his or her name forward.*

However, the designation of the Commission president by a parliamentary body need not make it a significantly more political institution. For example, the rules could state that the runner-up in the process of choosing the Commission president, who would come from a different political party, would become Commission vice president. And so long as all the other commissioners were appointed on a basis similar to the current model – chosen by national governments and endorsed by the European Parliament – the political complexion of the Commission would be as broad-based and diverse as it is today.[4]

Another objection to MEPs having a role in the election of the Commission president is often heard from governments that are not great fans of the Parliament, such as those in London and Paris. They fear that such an election would increase the Parliament's control over the Commission, relative to the governments. However, the reality today is that the Parliament already has considerable influence over commissioners, who cannot get their work done without gaining the confidence and support of MEPs. This is quite proper, for the Commission is answerable to both the Council of Ministers and the Parliament. It is good that there are two bodies watching the Commission. In any case, it is not self-evident that if MEPs shared a role with national MPs in the election of the president and vice president – once every five years – the Parliament would gain much more sway over the Commission.

Just as the Congress should give some popular legitimacy to the appointment of the European Council chairman, by voting him or her in, it is equally important that the European Council be involved in the election of the Commission president (and vice president). After all, the heads of government will have to work with the Commission president, who is a member of the European Council. And a Commission president elected in this new manner is likely to be quite a powerful figure.

Two models are possible:

★ After the European elections the Congress would meet. Depending on the relative strengths of the parties among national MPs and MEPs, the Congress would make its choice for the Commission presidency. The European Council would then have the right to say yes or no. In normal circumstances it would be politically impossible for the heads of government to reject a name, unless it was someone like Jean-Marie Le Pen.

★ The European Council would decide on a short-list of approved names. It could choose one per political family, thus deciding the candidate of each European political party. Or it could try to minimise the appearance of control-freakery by approving several names for each party, leaving the parties free to designate one of the approved names as their candidate for the presidency. After the European elections, the Congress would meet and choose one name as the Commission president.

The advantage of the first model is its simplicity. The pan-European political parties would have complete freedom to choose their own candidates for the presidency. The problem with the second is that it is very *de haut en bas*. The fact that heads of government would be deciding who could run for the Commission presidency might increase voter cynicism. The only advantage of the second model is that the heads of government are more likely to accept it.

The Congress could also approve the EU's annual work programme. This should emerge every year out of consultations between the European Council, the High Representative and the Commission, and consist of three parts. First, the European Council chairman should, in co-operation with the members of that body (including the Commission president and the High Rep), draw up a general programme for the Union as a whole. This should consist of broad, strategic orientations. Second, under the supervision of the European Council, the High Representative should draw up a more detailed report and plan for the Union's foreign and security policy. And third, the Commission should work out a detailed report and plan for Community business, in line with the European Council's broad guidelines, and present it to the heads of government for their approval. The European Council chairman, the High Representative and the Commission president would each submit their plans to the Congress. After due debate, Congress would have to vote to approve them or not.

A single tower, not three pillars

This chapter has argued for a division of labour between the European Council, led by its chairman, and the Commission, led by its president. Such a division should not preclude a merger of the Union's three pillars. The creation of a single legal framework for the

EU would not mean the application of the Community method to foreign and defence policy, nor to co-operation on criminal justice and policing. Clearly, many governments would not want the Commission, Court of Justice or Parliament to play the kind of role in those areas that they do in traditional first-pillar business. Therefore within a single pillar, distinct decision-making procedures would apply to different sorts of activity, as is already the case within the first pillar.

But if the procedures continued to vary according to subject, what would be the point of collapsing the pillars? The answer is that in a single pillar, the institutions could become simpler, more transparent and more efficient. And in the long run a single pillar would make it easier for the EU to embrace more radical institutional reforms.

A merger of the EU's three pillars would allow it to have a legal personality. Currently, the Community is a legal entity, which can sign international agreements in areas where it has competence, such as foreign trade. But the second and third pillars are not legal entities, and if the EU wants an agreement with another country on, say, police co-operation or land-mines, every EU government has to sign and then ratify it.

With its own legal personality, the EU could become a little less confusing, particularly for those outside it. For example, many of the EU's international agreements – such as the trade and co-operation agreement currently under negotiation with Iran – are 'mixed': some sections are the competence of the Community, and some the competence of the member-states. If the EU could sign agreements in its own name, all the member-states would still have to approve the parts for which they had competence, for example in the case of Iran the provisions on human rights and weapons proliferation. However, after national ministers had signed the agreement, it would not require the approval of every member-state parliament, a process which often causes delay.

A merger of the pillars could help the efficiency and speed of decision-making. The division of foreign policy responsibilities between the first and second pillars, for example, currently creates needless complications. Take the imposition of EU sanctions on another country. The Council of Ministers takes a decision to apply sanctions through a unanimous, second-pillar procedure. But the Commission then has to propose a sanctions regime which the ministers vote upon by a qualified majority, according to a first pillar voting procedure. A single pillar could make it easier to see who is responsible for what, and reduce the risk of conflict among the institutions, for example over budgets. More fundamentally, the EU needs a legal personality before it can adopt the kind of constitutional text that Peter Hain advocates in the introduction to this volume.

Some federalists become very excited at the prospect of an EU legal personality. They imagine that, once all the EU's business is conducted within a single legal framework, there will be an inexorable tendency for the Community method to extend into every area. And they suppose that, sooner or later, the EU will replace its member governments in international organisations like the IMF and the United Nations.

The federalists should not get too excited. For any decision to give the EU a single treaty and legal personality would only lead to the 'communitisation' of a policy area if all the governments agreed that it should. The precise rules for, say, the conduct of EU defence policy, or for representation in the United Nations, would be decided, as at present, by the member governments. They would be unlikely to want radical changes. They might decide that, in some international bodies – such as those that deal with weapons proliferation – there would be value in EU representation alongside that of the member-states. And they might decide that the EU itself should sign the European Convention on Human Rights – or not.

However, any reduction of national parliamentary involvement should imply a greater role for EU institutions in scrutinising JHA measures. There are some specific reasons for putting all JHA matters in the first pilllar. At present, a third pillar agreement on JHA, such as that on the common arrest warrant, cannot enter into force until each member-state has pushed primary legislation through its national parliament. This may take many years. First-pillar laws can be implemented much more speedily: once the Council has passed a directive, national governments can transpose it directly through secondary legislation, which does not normally require parliamentary time.

At present the Commission, Court and Parliament are entirely excluded from some of the most inter-governmental dossiers, such as police co-operation. When the EU becomes involved in a policy area, some oversight at EU level is desirable, even if – as in CFSP or some parts of JHA – national governments remain pre-eminent. This is because there is sometimes little or no effective national oversight of decisions in these areas. For example the Parliament should be able to question the High Representative on EU foreign policy. And the Court of Justice should be able to review the application of EU law in Justice and Home Affairs, such as that concerning the new common arrest warrant (see Chapters 2 and 6). Therefore, if the creation of a single legal entity helps to diminish theological opposition to the involvement of EU institutions in those areas of policy-making which are primarily inter-governmental, so much the better.

In the longer run the case for more radical institutional reform may grow. The abolition of the pillars would make it easier for the EU to embark on major reforms, if and when the member-states consented to do so. For example, if the EU wanted to create its own diplomatic service, or to merge the jobs of Solana and Patten, it could not do so without first becoming a single legal entity.

Creating such an entity need not and should not shift the balance between inter-governmental and Community institutions. The success of the EU has depended on the balance between them. Jean Monnet understood the importance of the Union having these twin sources of authority: the European Coal and Steel Community that he created had both a High Authority (the forerunner of the Commission) and a Council of Ministers. The model suggested in this essay attempts to reflect that thinking: a strong Union requires a strong European Council chairman and a strong Commission president, each working within clearly defined boundaries.

Of course, the division between inter-governmental and Community decision-making leads to inefficiencies, particularly in the realm of foreign policy, as Chapter 2 makes clear. In the very long run, Europe should be able to evolve towards a single system of government, with the two sides blending into a single European administration. But for the time being such a step is not practical: for example, partisans of the Community method fear that attempts to merge Patten's job with Solana's would lead to an inter-governmental takeover; at the same time advocates of inter-governmental decision-making fear that a merger of those two jobs would lead to a Commission takeover. The paranoia and lack of confidence on both sides is extraordinary and to be regretted.

In the long run Europe's leaders will surely overcome these fears and manage to design a single system of governance. In the meantime, however, the existing institutional system – once simplified, clarified and reformed – offers a good model for providing the EU with leadership. As subsequent chapters show, there is much that can be done to bring the two sides closer together. For now, however, Europe needs a system of dual leadership.

★

Designing an exit door for the EU

In all the debates on the future of the European Union, there is one big problem that politicians and diplomats refuse to talk about, at least in public: the Union is finding it increasingly difficult to ensure that new treaties become law. Under current rules, no amendment to the treaties can enter into force until signed by every government, and then ratified by every member-state – either through parliamentary vote, or referendum, depending on the national procedure.

So when in 1992 the Danes voted 'no' to the Maastricht treaty, it could not become law until they changed their mind in a second referendum a year later. And then in June 2001 the Irish voted 'no' to the Nice treaty. If they voted 'no' a second time (this book went to press shortly before the October 2002 Irish referendum), the Nice treaty would be null and enlargement could be delayed. The votes of a nation of less than four million people would then have had a major impact on the 370 million other people in the EU, in addition to the 80 million preparing to join.

Assuming that the current round of enlargement is completed on time, with ten new members joining in 2004, the ratification of new treaties will become an even more daunting prospect. What if the 390,000 Maltese vote 'no' to the treaty that comes out of the Convention and the 2004 inter-governmental conference; or the 1.4 million Estonians? Must other Europeans abandon their plans for reforms that are designed to make the Union more democratic and efficient, simply because one small country does not like them?

Federalists have from time to time suggested that if a majority of the member-states ratified a new treaty, it should enter into force and the minority would have to grin and bear it. However, it is wishful thinking to suppose that a country whose parliament or people had voted 'no' to a new treaty – even one already signed by its government – would meekly accept such an alien imposition. The Commission has no tanks to deploy against recalcitrant countries, and it is not going to procure any.

But something must be done about the ratification problem. In the Convention there is widespread support for splitting the treaties into two, so that part one would be a constitutional document, setting out the aims and values of the EU, and its principal institutional arrangements. More detailed provisions for the EU's particular policies would go into a second part, which could be changed by a unanimous inter-governmental agreement and would not require ratification before entering into law.

Such a division of the treaties makes sense, assuming that national parliaments can be persuaded to give up their right to ratify changes to all parts of the treaties. But there would still be times when the first, constitutional part of the treaty needed changing.

So there needs to be a new procedure to make ratification easier. The proposal which follows would allow the overwhelming majority of EU citizens to push ahead with a treaty change, if they wished to, while at the same time respecting the sovereignty of individual nations which reject change.

As with the current system, any amendment to the treaties would need the unanimous agreement of the governments. Each member-state would then be required to ratify the change within 18 months. The treaty would enter into effect, so long as any countries that failed to ratify did not have populations amounting to 10 per cent or more of the EU's total population. That total is likely to be roughly 450 million after the next round of enlargement. Therefore one of the big four – Britain, France, Germany and Italy – would be able to block a treaty change on its own, as would a group of smaller countries with a combined population of 45 million. Then the treaty would become void.

The small countries might find it hard to swallow that a single large country could block a treaty change while a single small country could not. However, current decision-making procedures, many of which require uninamity, give the smalls a voting power that is disproportionate to the size of their populations. In an EU of 20 or more small countries, this will be harder and harder to justify. Under this new proposal, the votes of people from small countries would count as much as those from large countries. Any group of 45 million people would be able to block a treaty change, whether they lived in one large country or in several small ones.

Suppose, then, that a treaty change becomes law, after ratification in most EU countries, but that one or a few small countries withhold their approval. The country (or countries) concerned would then have two years to think again. During that time the government could negotiate any number of declarations with its EU partners, to clarify certain aspects of the treaty, perhaps to reassure its population. Or it could seek to negotiate an opt out from the new treaty.

Such an opt out would be viable only if it did not damage the effectiveness of the Union's common policies and institutions. For example, Denmark might wish to negotiate an opt out from the establishment of a European army; an army would work perfectly well without the Danes. But Denmark would not be allowed to opt out of the EU's trade or foreign policies, or from the basic institutional provisions that have to apply to all members.

If the country concerned is then able to ratify the new treaty, with added declarations or opt outs, the problem is solved. But if it cannot, it would be obliged to either leave the EU altogether, or enter the European Economic Area (EEA) to which Iceland, Liechtenstein and Norway belong. In essence they accept the rules of the EU's single market but have no vote on the making of EU laws. EEA members do not receive payments from the agricultural or regional policies, and do not participate in EU foreign policy.

What if the country obliged to leave was in the eurozone? Of course, a country that left the EU would be free to abandon the common currency. But if it wanted to stay in the euro – and for the sake of economic stability and foreign investment it may well wish to remain – it should be allowed to do so, so long as it met certain conditions.

On the face of it, it might seem odd for a country to be a member of the eurozone but not the EU itself. However, Norway and Iceland have signed up to the EU's Schengen agreement, under which they have no passport controls with other EU states, despite being outside the EU. The future institutional architecture of Europe is likely to include several such wrinkles and exceptions. The decision of a country not to integrate in one area should not prevent it from staying integrated in others, especially when – as is the case with the euro – disengagement would be likely to lead to real hardship for some companies and individuals.

A country that left the EU but kept the euro would need to stay in the EEA, so that its economy remained as integrated as possible with the other countries in the single currency. Such a country should be allowed the same representation and voting rights on the ECB Governing Council as other eurozone members (as Chapter 8 makes clear, after enlargement not all the central bank governors of eurozone members will be able to vote all the time). But this country would also have to accept the large quantity of EU legislation that is relevant to the euro system, for example on the excessive deficit procedure and the broad economic policy guidelines, without having a vote in the council of finance ministers. The finance minister of the country concerned would be a non-voting member of that council, and of the Euro Group. This country would also have to accept the jurisdiction of the European Court of Justice on these matters. If it found all this hard to accept, it would be free to leave the euro.

The EU needs an exit door not only for members that cannot digest treaty change, but also for any country that wishes to leave. Some Eurosceptics complain that, because the treaties contain no procedure for allowing a country to depart, there is no way out. Of course, that is incorrect. Britain would have left if the Eurosceptics had won its 1975 referendum. And Greenland did leave after holding a referendum in 1986.

But it would make sense to write an exit clause into the EU treaties, to remind everyone that the EU is a union of freely consenting states, and that divorce is always possible. The larger the EU grows, the more likely it is that one or more of its members will want to leave the club.

Charles Grant

2 Foreign and security policy: from bystander to actor
Steven Everts

★ If Europe's leaders want the EU to play a greater role in global diplomacy, they should abolish the rotating presidency; create a real foreign affairs council; and give a right of initiative to the High Representative for the Common Foreign and Security Policy, currently Javier Solana.

★ If the High Representative and the Commissioner for external relations agree on a joint a proposal, EU foreign ministers should take a vote. Such joint proposals would become effective if a qualified majority voted in favour.

★ The EU must also learn to use its wide-ranging set of instruments – such as policies on trade, aid, sanctions, migration and the environment – to support a clear political strategy. In particular, it should increasingly make its financial assistance conditional upon recipient countries respecting international standards on good governance, democratisation, non-proliferation and counter-terrorism.

★ Success in EU foreign policy depends on better co-operation between the member-states and EU institutions. The member-states should send more national diplomats to work for Solana in the Council secretariat, and to the Commission's overseas delegations. Over time, the EU should transform its delegations into EU embassies that are staffed by its own diplomatic service.

Foreign policy – broadly defined – should be the EU's next big project. While the EU is often unpopular, more than 75 per cent of its citizens want Europe to play a bigger role in world affairs. Whether the issue is the latest crisis in the Middle East, rising US unilateralism or on-going instability in Afghanistan, the question that echoes throughout the Union is always the same: what can Europe do? Both leaders and the public are deeply unhappy about the mismatch between the EU's impressive economic resources and its deficient diplomatic clout. Both also instinctively understand that European countries can only influence global trends by pooling their resources and putting out a united message.

So it is right that the Convention on the future of Europe is looking at how to improve the EU's performance in foreign policy. While Europe's international role and ambition were hardly mentioned in the Laeken declaration – the document which provided the broad parameters for the Convention – the issue has now acquired a new sense of urgency. It has become clearer since September 11th that the world is a fractious place, characterised by rising levels of political tension, and that it faces a new set of security challenges. There is an urgent need for a Europe that can help solve these problems – and not just issue declarations about them.

Concretely, EU leaders must meet four inter-related challenges. They should streamline decision-making on foreign policy; ensure greater coherence across the whole range of EU external relations; show more courage in promoting EU values; and learn to set clear priorities.

Streamline decision-making and give the High Representative more resources

The EU must urgently improve its ability to be able to act in the field of foreign policy. Despite some progress, EU foreign policy can still too often be summed up as 'too little, too late'. For a start, the EU should abolish the rotating presidency, which puts a different country in the EU's driving seat every six months. This system has led to an unacceptable lack of continuity and coherence across the full range of EU external relations. Frequently, countries holding the presidency cannot resist pushing their pet projects at the expense of long-standing EU policies. Non-Europeans, and not just Americans, are right to criticise the change of priorities and personnel that this baffling system produces. Javier Solana, the current High Representative for the CFSP, and his officials should take over the presidency's tasks of representing the EU externally, chairing CFSP working groups and Council meetings, and providing impetus and follow-up. EU foreign policy can no longer afford the harmful consequences of changing the presidency every six months.

The CFSP decision-making process also needs to become smoother, especially if the Union is to avoid total paralysis after enlargement. There is a real danger that EU decision-making will become even harder than it is today. Enlargement is set to bring in ten new countries as early as 2004 – each with its own peculiar views and domestic lobbies. It is clear that without reforms to the EU's decision-making structures, enlargement will make a bad situation even worse.

There are two ways in which the Union can safeguard its ability to act with 25 or more member-states. First, the EU should learn to overcome its near-obsession with unanimity. Of course, it is often preferable to act 'at 15'. But too often the EU's consensus fixation is producing mushy and anodyne positions that nobody really wants but everyone can accept. Interestingly, the treaties already allow implementation decisions to be taken by 'super' qualified majority voting (the threshold for QMV is higher in the CFSP than in other policy areas). Any attempt to radically broaden the scope of QMV in the CFSP will lead to strong opposition from, among others, the British, French, Swedish and Danish governments. But at the very least the EU should use those provisions already in the treaty – including 'constructive abstention' – to bypass the ability of one or a few member-states to delay, or water down, proposals that the vast majority of other member-states supports.

Second, the EU should use more informal leadership coalitions to prepare decisions in smaller, nimbler groups. In CFSP – as in other fields – an enlarged Union will have to find innovative ways of allowing variable leadership coalitions to emerge, and pull the whole Union forward. Membership in these informal groups should depend on the level of experience, resources and commitment that countries possess on a particular issue. It is certainly not axiomatic that the big countries will always play a leading role. Still, some smaller member-states will not like this idea, seeing it as a threat to their treaty-guaranteed position of equality vis-à-vis the other members. But the alternatives are constant drift and deadlock in EU foreign policy, because the big countries often cannot agree amongst themselves, or when they do agree, form an overt *directoire* outside EU structures. Informal leadership groups are the best way out.

Javier Solana has been a great success as Mr CFSP. He has put the EU on the map, in the Balkans, the Middle East and elsewhere. Some of the EU's modest foreign policy achievements in 2002, such as the agreement between Serbia and Montenegro or the deal on the Church of the Nativity in Bethlehem, are largely due to Solana's clever political manoeuvring. He clearly has the trust of all EU capitals – not just London, Paris and Berlin. The time has come to build on his successes. If the High Representative had a formal right of initiative, his position would be stronger. Foreign ministers acting in the Council would, of course, retain the final say. But the High Representative would be in a better position to initiate and push forward new policy ideas. However, the function of High Representative should be separated from that of the secretary-general of the Council. Clearly, the Solana figure should be central to EU foreign policy-making, but he needs to work full time on foreign policy.

Giving the High Representative a right of initiative would put him, in that respect, at the same level as the Commission and the member-states. It is clear that EU foreign policy would produce more impressive results if all sides worked better together – and if the EU could take decisions more easily. One way to achieve both these objectives would be to promote more joint initiatives. The EU should decide that if the High Representative and the commissioner for external relations agreed on a joint proposal, then EU foreign ministers should accept that initiative if a (super) qualified majority voted in favour. Because Solana has such excellent links with the capitals, he would filter out any idea that he knew was too controversial. Similarly, by involving the Commission at an early stage in the policy process, the EU could ensure that the damaging divide between the first and second pillar – between the 'money' and the diplomatic strategy – was reduced.

In any case, Mr CFSP needs more resources to function effectively. Tripling the CFSP budget (to €120 million) may sound ambitious, but it would stop Solana having to beg the member-states to give him the money to do what they have already asked him to do. So if the Council asked Solana to promote a peace settlement in the Middle East, he should have a budget for performing such tasks, for example by appointing additional special representatives or by paying for certain political initiatives. For instance, the EU has pledged financial help to a campaign by leading Palestinians who argued the case against suicide bombing and stressed that it was politically counter-productive. But it proved very hard to find the money.

More generally, EU leaders routinely pledge their support for a Union that is able to assert itself more strongly on the global stage. But then they balk at the financial consequences. The EU cannot develop a credible foreign policy 'on the cheap'. In terms of financial control, both the Council and the European Parliament – working with special procedures – should hold the High Representative accountable for his CFSP budget. Some officials in the Council secretariat campaign for a greater CFSP budget, but oppose giving the Parliament even a consultative role in financial oversight. Since the CFSP budget is part of the overall EU budget, such a position is not reasonable. The bargain should be: yes to a significant rise in the CFSP budget, but yes also to giving the European Parliament a scrutinising role.

For the time being, 'pure' defence spending should be kept separate from the regular EU budget. The EU should finance crisis management operations out of a new EU defence budget, rather than have individual member-states pay for operational expenses on a 'costs lie where they fall' basis (meaning that national governments pay for the contributions they make to EU missions). The current mechanism produces unseemly rows, encourages 'free riding' behaviour and is ripe for reform. Member-states should pay into this EU defence budget the equivalent of a very small fraction of their GDP. But, in contrast to the CFSP budget, the High Representative would be accountable for these expenses only to the Council, and thus indirectly to national parliaments. Over time, if the political conditions changed, the EU defence budget could be folded into the regular EU budget.

Apart from a greater, and more stable, budget, the Solana figure also needs more people working for him. The number of officials in both the policy unit, which has a medium-term planning function, and the Council's directorate-general for external relations should rise substantially. The Union can achieve this by stationing more national diplomats in both these parts of the Council secretariat – on short-term secondments and through direct recruitment.

Ensure better co-ordination across the whole range of EU external actions

Most criticism of the EU's international role focuses on the divisions among the member-states. Despite some progress, it is true that on certain issues – think of strategy towards Iraq – the member-states do not agree. But divisions among the EU institutions are equally damaging, and receive much less attention. Existing institutional arrangements for running EU foreign policy are confusing and overlapping. Responsibilities and resources are split between the Commission, the Council and the member-states. As a result, the proverbial left hand often does not know what the right hand is doing. Worse, sometimes the policies that one bit of the Brussels machinery pursues are directly at odds with the actions of other bodies.

Therefore, the EU should work harder to guarantee that its policies on trade, aid, Justice and Home Affairs and the environment are explicitly linked to the Union's foreign policy objectives. The General Affairs Council should ensure this sort of co-ordination, but the GAC no longer works well. Too often it gets bogged down in the minutiae of policy disputes that other councils have failed to solve. There is not enough time to discuss EU foreign policy issues in a strategic and pro-active manner. In place of the GAC the EU needs to set up an official foreign affairs council, made up of the 15 foreign ministers and with a clear focus on running EU external relations. A new body of senior ministers, appointed by prime ministers, could then concentrate on the internal EU agenda. At the Seville summit in June 2002, EU leaders went some way in this direction by turning the GAC into a new 'General Affairs and External Relations Council' (see Chapter 3 for more details).

The EU also needs to overcome the split between the supranational and the inter-governmental side of external policy, headed by the Commissioner for external relations and Mr CFSP respectively. There is too much distrust between the two bureaucracies, which hinders the sort of close co-ordination and mutual support that EU foreign policy requires. In the very long run – say 20 years – EU foreign policy should probably be run by a single foreign policy supremo, based in the Commission but answerable to the foreign ministers. In May 2002, Commission President Romano Prodi proposed to go even further, suggesting that this person should also have the sole right of initiative.

Clearly, most member-states are opposed to such radical ideas. Foreign policy questions are simply too sensitive. It is also hard to see why the Commission should claim a monopoly of good ideas on how to project EU values and interests worldwide. But one intermediate step that could gain wide support would be to make the next commissioner for external relations the deputy to the next High Representative. This would promote greater synergies between CFSP and the Union's common policies and instruments. Mr CFSP should also take part in most Commission meetings that deal with foreign affairs, while the commissioner for external relations should go to most meetings of the Political and Security Committee (the EU body of national diplomats that runs CFSP on a day-to-day basis). Another deputy ('Mr ESDP') could look after defence matters, with a brief to beef up Europe's underwhelming military capabilities (see box on page 46).

Moreover, the Commission's diplomatic representations abroad should expand their role in CFSP, reporting to both the High Representative and the Commission. Many more national diplomats and Council officials should be inserted into Commission delegations for short periods, where they should take the lead in promoting joint reporting. Over time, Commission delegations should evolve into EU embassies, staffed by EU diplomats servicing and representing the EU on foreign policy as well as on other issues. The point of all these measures would be to ensure greater coherence and consistency across the whole field of EU external policies.

In the medium term, the EU should create its own diplomatic service. The EU can develop a credible common foreign policy without becoming a single state. But to do so without the help of a corps of EU diplomats would be hard. EU citizens should be able to choose between joining their own national service or the EU service. EU diplomats, rather than national diplomats, should gradually take the lead in encouraging a shared perspective on international problems. The more member-states share analyses of common problems, the greater the chances that they will agree on the necessary policy responses.

Champion international organisations and make financial assistance more conditional

The EU is right to aim for an international system based on rules, plus international institutions that promote international co-operation and enforce compliance. Despite the claims of some Americans and other sceptics, promoting international rules and robust multilateral regimes is not a sign of weakness. Rather, strong rules and norms, plus independent verification and enforcement mechanisms, are necessary to solve many of the world's most pressing problems – particularly those relating to failed states, terrorism, weapons proliferation, organised crime and the environment. Of course, the EU should, whenever possible, try to work with the US, because this is nearly always a precondition for effective international action. At the same time, Europe should resist superpower envy and develop its own, distinctive approach to international affairs.

One area where the EU should do much better is in converting the vast amounts of money it spends abroad into more international influence. It should learn to leverage its trade and aid instruments, linking trade privileges and financial assistance to clear commitments from the recipient countries to promote political and economic reforms. The overwhelming consensus of development experts is that financial assistance will only make a lasting difference if the money is used to back reform-minded governments.

But linking aid flows to standards of good governance is not only sound advice from a development perspective. It is also clear since September 11th that messianic terrorism is fed by wells of hatred and disaffection throughout the greater Middle East and beyond. In turn, such anti-western feelings are often linked to Middle Eastern countries' unresponsive and sclerotic political systems, which fan the flames of religious and political extremism. For too long, Western policy towards the region has been reduced to a choice between backing authoritarian regimes or letting in the Islamic fundamentalist opposition. Forced to choose, the West has often preferred corruption to chaos. Both

Europe and the US now need to make the modernisation of the greater Middle East a top priority. The EU has plenty of resources and expertise, but it must learn to make its financial assistance more targeted and conditional. For example, projects that promote new channels of opposition, such as independent media or human rights groups, should receive a greater share of EU aid.

The EU should be firmer in insisting that promised reforms take place in the recipient countries. Interestingly, all the EU's 'partnership' or 'association' agreements with third countries contain clauses on respect for human rights, political pluralism and standards for good governance. These agreements should give the EU considerable influence, but ultra-cautious member-states are too often reluctant to invoke these clauses. That attitude should change. The EU should have the courage to link non-compliance with concrete actions, such as the postponement of new projects, a suspension of high-level contacts or the use of different channels of delivery (giving money to independent NGOs instead of government-run organisations). Using a benchmarking process, EU foreign ministers should reward countries which make progress in political and economic modernisation with extra EU and national assistance. But the EU should punish countries that fail to comply with the standards they themselves have pledged to uphold.

Set meaningful priorities and start with the 'near abroad'

EU foreign policy is a new and incomplete project. It badly needs clear priorities. EU politicians should therefore resist the temptation of dreaming up a common policy on all issues, conflicts and regions in the world. It is too early for such a comprehensive approach. In regional terms, the EU should be an active, outward-looking global player, and deepen its involvement in Asia, Africa and Latin America. But with the EU foreign policy still in its infancy, it would be wise to focus attention on the Balkans, Russia, Ukraine, the Middle East and North Africa. These regions contain many failed or failing states that together constitute an 'arc of instability' right on the EU's doorstep. The EU should make it a priority to develop agile and effective policies for these countries. The effort of tackling the security and economic problems of the Union's immediate vicinity should be a test-case for its ability to deploy its policy instruments and programmes in a joined-up way.

Convention members and EU leaders face a clear choice. Europe can either continue with lowest-common denominator policies, often complaining about America's go-it-alone tendencies, but never able to push for its own vision of how to tackle the world's problems. Or it can decide that it really wants a credible EU foreign policy, and accept the need for significant, if sometimes painful, reforms.

★

Time for Mr ESDP?

The EU's attempt to create a viable defence policy – born of Franco-British parentage at Saint Malo four years ago – has, so far, made only limited progress. A dispute between the Greek and Turkish governments has held up an agreement that would allow the EU access to NATO assets, while European efforts to increase military capabilities have produced only meagre results.

At present, the European Security and Defence Policy (ESDP) is part of the portfolio of Javier Solana, who became High Representative for the Common Foreign and Security Policy in 1999. Solana has proven his worth, for example in helping to cajole EU member-states into common foreign policy positions, and in negotiating settlements in Macedonia, and between Serbia and Montenegro. However, Solana has neither the time nor the resources to make a significant impact on European defence. National governments require both foreign ministers and defence ministers. Similarly, the EU member-states should give Solana a deputy to promote the ESDP.

Solana's deputy – 'Mr ESDP' – should manage the EU's military staff (now 120 strong) and sit on both the EU Military Committee (consisting of senior military officers) and the Political and Security Committee (consisting of national diplomats based in Brussels). In particular, Mr ESDP should take on the crucial role of pushing for more effective military capabilities. He should press the member-states to meet their promised contributions towards the EU's equipment goals. Every year he should publish a progress report on the EU's military assets, and then name and shame those governments that fail to fulfil their commitments.

Mr ESDP should also chair regular meetings of the EU defence ministers. European defence ministers already meet informally. However, the EU should create a formal council for defence ministers, which would meet on a regular basis. This council would encourage peer group pressure among the defence ministers, and more generally help to educate national defence ministries in the workings of the EU.

Another role for Mr ESDP would be to manage the crucial relationship between the EU and NATO. Most of the EU's military operations are likely to depend on NATO assets, such as its military planners, for the foreseeable future. To ensure that NATO is willing and able to lend its assets when they are needed, Mr ESDP will need to establish close ties to NATO's secretary-general. When Solana is too busy to attend meetings of the NATO council, Mr ESDP should represent the EU. And during a crisis, when Solana may be engaged in diplomacy with governments outside the EU, the member-states cannot expect him to also ensure that military preparations are running smoothly. Mr ESDP would be the appropriate person to liaise with national defence ministries.

In the longer term, Mr ESDP should devote some time to improving European armaments co-operation. He could start by encouraging national governments to co-ordinate their spending on military research and development. He should work closely with NATO to encourage European governments to harmonise their requirements for military equipment, and in some cases to develop specialised roles. Also, Mr ESDP could help stimulate competition among defence suppliers by promoting a Europe-wide defence market.

Finally, part of the new job should be to assess the suitability of the EU's military doctrine and institutions for the challenges it faces. The so-called Petersberg tasks set the parameters for EU military missions, which range from humanitarian relief to ending regional conflicts. But in the years to come, the EU may wish to develop the organisation and the capabilities to combat threats like terrorism and the proliferation of weapons of mass destruction, which are not covered by the Petersberg tasks. Mr ESDP's job would be to make the case for change to the defence ministers.

Solana has proven effective, despite having few formal powers, because of his tact and skills in dealing with the EU foreign ministers. Similarly, Mr ESDP need not have many formal powers vis-à-vis the defence ministers. But in order to be effective he would need ample experience of military matters, and the personality to command respect. Former defence ministers such as Alain Richard of France or Michael Portillo of Britain, would be possible candidates. Javier Solana, along with the EU foreign ministers, would still retain overall responsibility for the ESDP. But the creation of a Mr ESDP would lessen the workload of the already overburdened Solana, and help to strengthen the credibility of EU defence policy.

Daniel Keohane

3   A strategic European Council, a streamlined Council of Ministers
Charles Grant

★ The original purpose of the European Council needs to be restored: heads of government should be able to meet in an informal setting to discuss strategic issues. Two reforms would help: the creation of a new General Affairs Council (GAC), consisting of senior ministers appointed by prime ministers, to consider general EU business; and the abolition of the rotating presidency.

★ Within the Council of Ministers, four 'super-councils' would co-ordinate the work of the other ministerial formations: the GAC, chaired by the Commission president; the foreign affairs council, chaired by the High Representative; the council of finance ministers; and the council of interior ministers. The latter two would elect one of their number as chair.

★ The Council of Ministers should take decisions by the so-called double majority system: a measure would pass if a simple majority of the member-states, and a majority of the EU's population – represented by governments – were in favour.

★ Among reforms that do not require treaty change, the European Council should abandon the principle that its decisions always require unanimity. And the Council of Ministers should be open to the public when considering legislation.

The problems in the European Council – the regular summits of heads of government – and the Council of Ministers are less widely known than those in the European Commission, but just as serious. Indeed, the inefficiencies of these two bodies, which together represent the interests of national governments in the EU, have contributed to the lack of leadership from which the Union currently suffers. The Seville summit in June 2002 agreed to some modest reforms, but these are only a very small step in the right direction.

Valéry Giscard d'Estaing, then the French president, invented the European Council in 1974. As the EU's supreme authority, it has proved decisive on subjects such as the creation of the euro, past enlargements of the Union, and revisions of the treaties. It includes the president of the European Commission and now meets every three months.

The point of the European Council is to allow prime ministers to think about big, long-term issues in an informal atmosphere. But these days it seldom fulfils that role. The Barcelona and Seville summits of 2002 were not as embarrassing as the Laeken summit of December 2001, when prime ministers shouted abuse at each other over the location of a food safety agency. Worse still was the Nice summit of December 2000, which dragged on for four days and nights because of a failure to reach an agreement on the distribution of votes among the various countries in the Council of Ministers.

The presidency of the European Council shifts from one EU government to another every six months. The rotating presidency also chairs the many sectoral formations of the Council of Ministers (the trade ministers, the environment ministers, and so on), as well as the hundreds of committees and working groups in which officials take decisions.

The rotating presidency and the General Affairs Council (the GAC, consisting of the foreign ministers) have had the joint task of preparing summits and are supposed to ensure that the heads of government deal with only the crucial subjects. However, the foreign ministers have to struggle with world events as much as the EU's general business and are usually more interested in the former. In recent years they have frequently failed to prepare summits properly.

Meanwhile, as Chapter 1 explained, the institution of the rotating presidency is rapidly losing credibility. The country with the presidency has to chair every EU meeting as well as plan summits and represent its own national interests, and the key officials often cannot cope with the strain.

Because summits are under-prepared, many disputes on minor matters go to the prime ministers for resolution. But they cannot always settle them: by tradition, decisions of the European Council require unanimity. For example, the Laeken summit tried but failed to resolve arguments over an EU patent and the Galileo satellite project.

Each summit also has to approve a swathe of reports and documents that the prime ministers will not have read. They spend a lot of time revising the very detailed summit conclusions, the drafts of which are written by officials before the prime ministers gather. These conclusions, which tend to cover every conceivable problem in every part of the world and often run to novella length, have a quasi-judicial status. With hundreds of officials milling around, the intimacy and informality of Giscard's original concept is lost. Enlargement will soon bring another ten delegations to each meeting, making them even more cumbersome.

The regular meetings of EU ministers are often little more effective than those of the prime ministers. The system of *tours de tables* means that every minister takes it in turn to speak, often with a notable lack of concision. Once every minister has read out his or her opening statement, there may be little time left for genuine debate, and it is not surprising that the more senior ministers often send their deputies.

The plethora of separate ministerial councils – 16 with a formal status until the Seville summit – has reduced the effectiveness of the Council of Ministers as a whole. Each group of ministers has its own priorities and likes to legislate, sometimes in contradiction to the priorities of other councils. The environment ministers, for example, have a tendency to create extra regulations, sometimes exasperating the industry ministers, whose job is to reduce red tape. Neither the rotating presidency nor the GAC has a good record of co-ordinating the work of the various councils.

Another problem is that the Council of Ministers and the Commission remain disconnected. Sharing responsibility for the EU's executive action, each is inclined to waste energy on turf wars with the other. The lack of co-ordination between the two sometimes makes it hard for the EU to produce coherent policies, especially in external relations. They need to find ways of working together more closely, in a pragmatic, results-driven spirit.

Pressure for change

The European Council, the Council of Ministers and the rotating presidency all need serious reform. Some of the reforms that are necessary – particularly those which concern the presidency – will require treaty change, and must await the next opportunity in 2004. However the heads of government could begin work on a number of reforms, within the framework of the existing treaties.

In February 2002 Tony Blair and Gerhard Schröder proposed a series of sensible reforms that would not require treaty change. Their joint letter called for the introduction of qualified majority voting (QMV) in the European Council for those matters which the Council of Ministers already decides by QMV. This could apply, for example, to issues such as energy liberalisation or some reforms of EU farm policy. Since the introduction of QMV for single market legislation in the late 1980s, votes have occurred only rarely. Nevertheless, the threat of being out-voted encourages ministers to make compromises and trade-offs, and the results have been positive. The use of QMV in the European Council would similarly encourage heads of government to seek compromises.

In March 2002, Javier Solana – who has the jobs of both secretary-general of the Council of Ministers and High Representative for foreign policy – produced his own proposals for reform. The most significant was for a new General Affairs Council to tackle the 'horizontal' matters – such as institutional questions, enlargement and summit preparations – which cut across the various sectoral councils. He suggested that the new GAC consist of deputy prime ministers, or ministers for European affairs, or that the existing GAC could be split into two formations – one for external affairs and one for general issues.

Solana is right that the key to a more focused and strategic European Council is a new GAC. This council should consist of senior ministers appointed by prime ministers, with the clout to take on colleagues in sectoral councils. These ministers should spend a large part of their time in Brussels, which would help them to develop a better relationship with the Commission. The GAC should have a high public profile, helping to show the citizens of Europe that it is elected ministers, rather than unelected bureaucrats, who take most of the key decisions in the EU.

The Seville reforms

The Seville summit in June 2002 agreed to a series of reforms, though they were less ambitious than those envisaged by Solana, Blair and Schröder. President Chirac blocked the idea of the European Council voting by QMV – fearing that it could be used against France on farm policy reform or energy liberalisation. Some small countries such as Portugal, worried about any dilution of the national veto, supported France in this blocking manoeuvre.

To improve the efficiency of summits, EU leaders decided that in future, meetings on the margins with third states or organisations would be held "in exceptional circumstances only". Each delegation will be limited to two seats in the meeting room, and the total size of a national delegation will be no more than 20. That is a radical change: many national delegations have consisted of a hundred or more officials.

The European Council decided that henceforth it will adopt, on the basis of consultations with the Commission and the presidencies concerned, a three-year strategic programme for the Union. This is, potentially, an important change. Blair had floated the idea of the European Council setting guidelines for the Commission and the Council of Ministers in his Warsaw speech of October 2000, but this had met opposition, especially from countries which fear any reduction of the Commission's independence.

Several small countries objected to the idea of splitting the GAC into two: some foreign ministers believed that a split would reduce the importance of their jobs, despite the fact that any member-state would be free to send the same minister to each council, if it wished. More generally, some small countries appeared to view this as another scheme to strengthen the role of the big countries. Yet it is hard to see how a more effective GAC would harm the interests of the small countries, unless they are opposed to an effective Council per se, which is presumably not the case.

So the compromise agreed in Seville was based on Solana's third option: the GAC would become the 'General Affairs and External Relations Council' (GAERC). This would have two formations:

★ One that prepares meetings of the European Council, follows up on its decisions, deals with institutional issues and manages 'horizontal' problems that cut across the sectoral councils.

★ And one that decides policy on the Union's external relations, including trade and aid.

The two formations will "hold separate meetings (with separate agendas and possibly on different dates)," and governments will be free to send different – or the same – people to the two sides of the GAERC. The ambiguous wording of Seville certainly allows the creation of what would be de facto a new GAC, based around Europe ministers rather than foreign ministers, but does not ensure that outcome.

After much argument, the summit decided to cut the number of sectoral councils from 16 to nine. Council debates on legislation that is subject to the co-decision procedure will be open to the public during the initial stage, when the Commission presents its proposals; and at the final stage, when ministers vote. To speed up meetings, the European Council said that it would encourage presidencies to control the order and length of ministerial interventions. As with so many of the Seville conclusions, this wording is a fudge: a strong presidency might use it as a justification for ending *tours de tables*, but that outcome is far from assured. Many smaller states are attached to the *tours*.

Streamlining the Council of Ministers

The Seville reforms do not go nearly far enough. The Council should be fully open to the public when in legislative mode, if it wants its pretensions to transparency to be taken seriously. And the ambiguity surrounding the GAERC needs to be resolved, so that it is quite clear that the EU has created a new body concerned with general EU questions, rather than an add-on to the regular meetings of foreign ministers.

Equally, proponents of majority voting in the European Council need to put this back on the agenda. The arrival of ten new prime ministers after enlargement will strengthen their case. However, according to one line of reasoning among Council of Ministers lawyers, there is no need for a formal decision on majority voting at summits. A strong presidency could do what Italian Prime Minister Bettino Craxi did at Milan in 1985: when Mrs Thatcher opposed the calling of an inter-governmental conference to revise the treaties, he insisted on a majority vote under the rules that applied to the Council of Ministers, and she lost.

As argued in Chapter 1, there is a strong case for an individual, probably a former prime minister, to chair the European Council. With successive waves of enlargement bringing ever more prime ministers around the summit table, the European Council will require some leadership. The new chairman should focus the discussion on the key points, broker compromises and subsequently work to ensure the implementation of summit conclusions.

However, there is a case for retaining one aspect of the existing, rotating chairmanship. The presence of an EU summit in a particular member-state helps to give the Union – which generally appears to be distant – some real tangibility. If the citizens of a country see the heads of government arriving in one of their cities, they are more likely to take an interest in and develop some understanding of the EU. The Nice summit decided that all formal European Councils should in future meet in Brussels. That decision should be reversed, so that those countries which wish to host a summit are able to do so, by rotation.

Nine formations of the Council of Ministers are still too many. There need be no more than four, but they would have to have a special 'super-council' status. Even a new, strong GAC is not going to be able to oversee the finance ministers' council (Ecofin). With the coming of the euro, Ecofin has become increasingly influential. Finance ministers such as Gordon Brown, Hans Eichel or Francis Mer will not want the GAC to co-ordinate their policies with those of other councils.

Therefore Ecofin needs 'super-council' status, alongside the new GAC. A third super-council should be for foreign affairs. Freed of their general responsibilities, the foreign ministers could focus exclusively on foreign policy. The fourth and final super-council should be that of the interior ministers, who cover the expanding dossiers of Justice and Home Affairs.

Without a rotating presidency, who would chair these bodies? The Commission president should chair the GAC. This would help to ensure that the Commission and the GAC worked together in co-ordinating the work of the other councils and in preparing for summits. The foreign affairs council needs a full-time chairman. Therefore the High Representative, who is appointed by the heads of government, should chair the foreign ministers' meetings. He should also assume the core external functions of the rotating presidency.

Ecofin and the JHA council do not – for the time being – need a full-time, high-level representative. They should each elect one of their number as chairman, for a period of say two-and-a-half years. There are precedents: both the Economic and Financial Committee, of senior officials, and the EU Military Committee of generals choose their own chair. The chair of Ecofin should also chair the Euro Group, the informal ministerial council for euro business, to ensure smooth links between the two bodies. If the Euro Group became a formal institution, it should report to the European Council through Ecofin, in which all its ministers sit.

A key task for the super-councils should be to prepare meetings of the European Council, with the onus on ensuring that heads of government deal with the minimum of paperwork. Between meetings of the European Council, the super-councils should work with the new chairman of the European Council and the Commission to ensure that the Union follows a clear and coherent strategy. The European Council would still have to sort out any disputes among the four super-councils – but that is a big advance on the post-Seville situation, when a summit may have to sort out the problems of up to nine formations.

The remaining sectoral councils would become 'sub-councils', acting as sub-committees of the super-councils. The GAC would co-ordinate their work, except when economic financial issues were to the fore, when Ecofin would do the job. The super-councils should have the power to ensure that the decisions of sub-councils were consistent and, if necessary, to over-rule those bodies. The chairmen of the Ecofin, foreign and JHA super-councils should become formal members of the European Council (the Commission president, who would chair the GAC, is already a member). Those four figures would become the transmission channels for implementing summit decisions and guidelines.

The Commission needs to be intimately involved in the Council of Ministers' decision-making procedures, so that it works with rather than against it. Therefore the relevant commissioner – for agriculture, social affairs or whatever – should chair each sub-council. However, the Commission has little role in military matters, so the defence ministers should elect one of their number as chairman of their sub-council, which would report to the foreign ministers; but if (as Chapter 2 suggests) the EU creates the post of 'Mr ESDP', as in European Security and Defence Policy, he or she should chair those meetings.

Ending the rotation, and new voting rules

The formal abolition of the rotating presidency would require a treaty change. As explained in Chapter 1, some small countries want to maintain the rotation. One compromise idea promoted by Sweden is that of team presidencies: instead of one country presiding, a group including both large and small countries would do so. Five countries, say, would divide up the various councils of ministers between them.

This scheme would deal with the difficulty that some of the future members may lack the capacity to run a presidency on their own. And it would reduce the heavy workload that now afflicts all presidencies. However, many of the problems of the rotating presidency would remain, such as a lack of continuity in external representation, and the temptation to push national priorities from the chair (would France be relaxed if Britain, as part of a five-country team, ended up chairing the agriculture council?). Meanwhile there would be the additional difficulty of five governments trying to co-ordinate the work of all the councils, presumably through some sort of steering committee. It would be much better to dispense with the rotating presidency altogether. The many working groups and low-level committees could be chaired by officials from the Commission or the Council secretariat, depending on the subject.

Finally, the Council of Ministers needs to rethink its mechanism for taking decisions. The problem with the new system of qualifed majority voting agreed at Nice is that no one except for experts in EU law understands it: in order to pass through the Council, a measure requires a) a qualified majority, defined as at least 74.1 per cent of the weighted votes; b) the support of a simple majority of member-states; and c) the support of member-states with populations amounting to 62 per cent of the EU's total population.

A much simpler method would be the 'double-majority', according to which the Council would pass a measure if a simple majority of the member-states and a majority of the EU's population – represented by their national government – were in favour. The first threshold safeguards the interests of the smaller countries, and the second the interests of the larger ones. France (plus Britain, Italy, Poland and Spain) would have to accept that Germany, with its 82 million people, had more clout in the Council. France's reluctance to lose parity with Germany is one reason why it resisted the double majority system at Nice. The population threshold could be set at a figure such as 50 or 60 per cent. The fact that this double majority system would be comprehensible to most voters should not – hopefully – rule out its adoption by the next inter-governmental conference.

The EU's governments will find it difficult to accept many of the reform proposals in this essay. But they have a clear self-interest in restoring the European Council's strategic purpose, and in streamlining the Council of Ministers. For these are the bodies which feed national interests into the EU decision-making process. The less efficient these inter-governmental institutions, the stronger the case for extending the powers of the EU's supranational bodies.

★

4 Economic reform: closing the delivery deficit
Alasdair Murray

★ The council of finance ministers should assume leadership of the EU's efforts on economic reform. Ecofin should become a 'super-council', co-ordinating all the Union's economic policy-making.

★ The EU should merge the plethora of specialist industry councils into an 'enterprise council', composed of European industry or economics ministers. The enterprise council should push forward structural reform, placing a special emphasis on improving the environment for entrepreneurs and small businesses.

★ The Commission should appoint a 'Lisbon commissioner' to oversee its own work on economic reform.

The EU has set itself a series of highly ambitious economic goals to fulfil in the next decade. Eurozone countries are committed to ensuring the long-term health of the single currency, which will mean further economic integration. The Union will need to incorporate successfully at least ten dynamic but diverse accession country economies. Above all, the EU is determined to meet the target, set in Lisbon in 2000, of becoming the 'world's most competitive knowledge-based economy' by 2010.

However, the EU's existing institutional structure appears inadequate to cope with these economic challenges. The EU has so far made only patchy progress towards meeting the Lisbon goals. At the Barcelona summit in March 2002, EU leaders again failed to make substantial headway – despite Tony Blair's insistence that it was a 'make or break' meeting for economic reform. Moreover, budgetary co-operation between eurozone countries appears to be faltering. The German government succeeded in the spring of 2002 in watering down a formal Commission warning about the state of its public finances. Then in June 2002, the new French government effectively reneged on a previous commitment to bring its budget into balance by 2004. Four eurozone countries, including France and Germany, are in danger of breaching the Stability and Growth Pact deficit ceiling in 2002. Clearly, eurozone countries urgently need to reconsider the policy framework for the single currency, and especially the terms of the Pact. However, the rewriting of the Stability and Growth Pact is primarily an issue of economic policy, not institutional reform, and is therefore beyond the scope of this pamphlet.

The 'Lisbon agenda', in particular, poses a new set of problems to the EU's traditional way of taking decisions. The EU has set out a broad reform programme, which could influence almost every aspect of the member-states' economic and social structures. The EU will need to employ a mixture of policy measures to achieve its Lisbon goals. The Union must not just improve the quality of single market legislation, based on the traditional 'Community method'. It must also make better use of the 'open method of co-ordination' – the EU's recently developed system of target-setting, benchmarking and peer pressure.

The imminent enlargement of the Union is likely to exacerbate the problems the EU faces in turning its rhetoric on economic reform into reality. With 15 members, the EU already finds it extremely difficult to reach a common position on many economic issues. The EU has still not reached agreement on vital pieces of legislation, such as the takeover directive – despite a decade of trying. Soon there will be up to ten new member-states, each with its own political sensitivities and economic idiosyncrasies which will need to be taken into account.

In May 2002, the Commission suggested that the Community method should be strengthened for eurozone budgetary policies. However, the Commission was silent on what institutional reforms are needed to ensure the EU can make real progress towards its Lisbon goals.

The Commission plays a vital role in drawing up single market measures and providing intellectual support to the Council of Ministers. However, significant progress towards the Lisbon targets requires intensified co-operation, both on the Community and open method sides of the economic reform programme. This requires the Council of Ministers to function more efficiently. Member-state governments took some first steps towards reform of the Council in June 2002, including a reduction in the number of specialist councils. But there are still far too many separate councils, meaning that there may be little or no coherence between overlapping initiatives. And the reforms did not tackle the problems of the six-monthly rotating presidency, which too often leads to a lack of policy continuity.

A stronger role for Ecofin

If the EU is going to deliver on its economic promises, it needs to move the council of finance ministers (Ecofin) centre-stage in the reform process. Only finance ministers have the political clout within their governments to deliver on the full range of Lisbon targets. In many European governments, finance ministers act as deputy prime ministers in all but name, using their control of the nation's purse-strings to influence the policies of other ministers.

Moreover, only Ecofin can restore coherence between EU micro-economic and macro-economic policies. Structural economic reforms, including the overhaul of labour and product markets, are vital to ensuring the long-term health of the single currency in particular and the EU economy in general. A concerted European economic reform effort would enable the EU to raise its long-term growth rates. And improved growth would help to reduce unemployment, making it easier for eurozone governments to meet the fiscal constraints of the Stability and Growth Pact.

The existing system of the rotating presidency means that difficult political issues, such as tax policy, tend to drop on and off the agenda, depending on the priorities of the minister in the chair. Instead, finance ministers should elect their own permanent chair. This modest reform would greatly improve policy continuity without further complicating the EU's institutional structure. The chair, who should serve for a period of two-and-a-half-years, would be responsible for drawing up the Ecofin agenda and for helping finance ministers deliver on their agreed policy goals. The chair should also work closely with the economics and monetary affairs commissioner, on reviewing eurozone budgetary policies. The priority should be to refine the workings of the Stability and Growth Pact, in a less rigid direction, rather than increase the Commission's powers to bring member-states into line.[5]

[5] See 'The EU needs a flexible pact', Alasdair Murray, CER Bulletin Issue 23, April-May 2002.

So long as there remains a distinction between the Euro Group, the informal council for eurozone finance ministers, and Ecofin, the Ecofin chair should hail from a eurozone country and oversee both formations. The election of separate chairs for each group would hamper co-ordination between EU macro and micro-economic policies. If there were a single elected chair for both formations of finance ministers, the case for granting the Euro Group formal legislative power – as the Commission proposes – would be weakened. A single chair would ensure that key Euro Group legislative issues could quickly be placed on the full Ecofin agenda. The creation of a formal Euro Group would also prove politically divisive, particularly in an expanded EU where a large number of member-states are likely to be, initially at least, outside the euro.

The new chair should consider two specific innovations to help improve the continuity and transparency of Ecofin decision-making. First, the chair should prepare an annual list of overall goals, with the agreement of the finance ministers and the support of the Commission. The European Parliament should have the opportunity to question the chair about the choice of goals and to monitor progress across the course of the year.

Second, the chair should lead Ecofin in an assessment of the Lisbon agenda, ahead of the EU's spring European Council which deals with economic issues. This should involve not just a review of progress in areas that are strictly the preserve of Ecofin, such as financial services or labour market issues, but also the relevant work conducted by other councils.

An economics 'super-council'

As Chapter 3 suggests, Ecofin should become a 'super-council', taking on the over-arching authority of the existing General Affairs Council, but only on economic issues. This means that Ecofin should oversee the other sectoral councils, such as the specialist single market formations, which have an economic dimension. Finance ministers should be able to try and broker deals on energy and postal liberalisation, for example, if their ministerial colleagues fail, rather than leaving these often complex issues to the heads of governments in the European Council. In effect, Ecofin should become the clearing-house for the Lisbon economic reform programme.

In return for this formal super-council role, finance ministers should cease to attend the European Council itself. This would have two direct benefits: first, it would reduce the number of ministers and officials attending summits, helping to restore their informality, and second, it would increase the pressure on Ecofin to reach agreement ahead of a summit. After all, this would be the only way that finance ministers could take political credit for progress on important issues.

However, one Ecofin representative – the elected chair – should continue to attend any summit where economic issues are discussed. The chair should present Ecofin's recommendations to the heads of government and deliver the Lisbon assessment report at the spring European Council. The chair would also be responsible for communicating to the finance ministers the strategic goals agreed by the summit.

An 'enterprise council'

Ecofin's reconstitution as a super-council, combined with the election of a chair, should help to ensure greater strategic leadership and co-ordination on economic policy issues. However, further progress on the EU's ambitious economic agenda will require other councils to play an important supporting role. In particular, the several councils covering internal market issues – such as energy and telecoms – continue to conduct vital work.

But the EU possesses far too many specialist councils for effective decision-making. Rather than continuing with a plethora of single market and industry-related councils, the EU should merge them into a single 'enterprise council', under the guidance of industry or economy ministers.

EU leaders took a first step in this direction at the Seville summit in June 2002. Heads of government agreed to merge the internal market, industry and research into a single 'competitiveness council'. However, separate councils will continue to meet for transport, telecoms and energy issues. The danger with this solution is that sectoral issues such as telecoms or energy liberalisation will continue to be considered in isolation from related economic reform issues.

The establishment of an enterprise council would bring distinct benefits to the EU economic policy process. First, it would enable the EU to develop a more coherent approach to business-related policy-making. The council should focus on all those micro-economic reforms, such as the liberalisation of the utilities sector, which could improve the underlying competitiveness of the European economy. But the council should also take the lead on initiatives designed to encourage entrepreneurs and improve the environment for small businesses. An enterprise council should be better able to develop a meaningful system of benchmarks and targets to achieve these goals.

Secondly, one senior minister in each member-state should in future take full responsibility for overseeing this part of the EU's economic reform agenda. Industry ministers often enjoy a high political standing within their own governments, but they have not had a clear-cut role on the European scene. The creation of an enterprise council would ensure that industry ministers developed 'ownership' of this aspect of the EU's agenda. Moreover, a powerful enterprise council would provide a political counter-weight to a stronger Ecofin. Ecofin would have the right to arbitrate when the enterprise council failed to reach agreement on key reforms. But the EU would greatly benefit from having a single council working full-time on business and competitiveness issues.

A 'Lisbon commissioner'

The reform of the EU's economic councils should not diminish the power of the Commission. On the contrary, the Commission will continue to play a pivotal role in preparing legislation and, increasingly, developing benchmarks and targets for the member-states to pursue.

At present, responsibility for economic reform issues is split between a number of commissioners – those for social affairs, the single market, enterprise, and energy and transport. If member-states ratify the Nice treaty, the number of commissioners working on economic policy is likely to increase even further. EU heads of government agreed at Nice to permit each country to appoint one commissioner, meaning that the Commission president will have to find portfolios for up to 25 commissioners after enlargement. Such a large Commission will be unwieldy and difficult to manage. In June 2002, Romano Prodi suggested that these problems could be overcome if the Commission president appointed an inner core of vice-presidents to steer the Commission's work programme. This makes sense: one of Prodi's inner group should oversee the Commission's work on economic reform.

The new 'Lisbon commissioner' should work in tandem with the chair of Ecofin to ensure that the EU's strategic economic targets are fulfilled. The commissioner should monitor the progress of the various Commission directorates-general in meeting their legislative goals. He or she should also refine and develop the Commission's approach to the non-legislative elements of the reform programme.

The Commission continues to have an ambivalent attitude towards those aspects of policy-making which fall outside the scope of the traditional Community method. However, the open method of co-ordination is often the only mechanism that is suitable for making progress on economic reform. The Commission should be leading attempts to improve the EU's efforts at co-ordinating economic policy in this fashion. Only the Commission possesses the resources, and the independence, to ensure that the open method finally becomes a powerful tool for European economic reform.

★

5 Modernising the European Commission
Ben Hall

★ The Commission should not gain new powers except in the field of crime and immigration, where there is a clear case for Community legislation. However, in an enlarged EU it is crucial that the Commission performs its existing role more effectively and, in particular, places more emphasis on the enforcement of EU rules.

★ The election of the Commission president would enhance not only its legitimacy, but also its credibility in dealings with the member-states.

★ The Commission should accelerate its efforts at internal reform. It should further modernise its budget management procedures and recruit more staff from national governments and the private sector.

A larger, more diverse community of states requires a stronger executive power at the centre. An authoritative European Commission is essential to enforce rules, to ensure that the big states do not brush aside the interests of small countries, and to seek genuinely common solutions to common problems. But the Commission must also become more accountable, to enhance the legitimacy of the European Union.

The balance of power between the supranational Commission and the inter-governmental Council of Ministers is the defining issue of the debate on the future of Europe. In recent years that balance has tipped strongly in favour of the Council.[6] The Commission has lost the political authority it enjoyed under its former president Jacques Delors. National leaders are less enthusiastic about entrusting it with new powers, preferring to co-operate among themselves on issues they consider to be at the core of national sovereignty. Some redressment is needed, in the Commission's favour.

[6] See 'What future for federalism?', Gilles Andréani, CER, September 2002.

However, the old federalist idea that the Commission should evolve into an executive government for Europe seems more fanciful than ever. Instead, the EU should retain its triangular structure of Commission, Council and Parliament, with executive power shared between the Commission and the Council. Meanwhile, the responsibility for implementing most EU policies should continue to be divided, as now, among the national capitals and Brussels.

The Commission should certainly not become a mere secretariat. If it is to act in the broad European interest – when it initiates legislation, regulates the single market or negotiates on the EU's behalf – it must continue to enjoy a high degree of autonomy from national governments. That executive freedom – embodied in the Commission's 'sole' right of initiative and its extensive regulatory powers – is the secret of the EU's success over the last 50 years.

However, the Commission's legal power to take action does not automatically make it an authoritative executive. Too often in the past, the Commission secured new responsibilities, irrespective of whether it had the administrative resources, the technical expertise or the political credibility to fulfil them. For example, the Commission has run the EU's technical assistance programme for the countries of the former Soviet Union, known as Tacis, with astonishing inefficiency. Moreover, the Commission's humiliating resignation in 1999 demonstrated that it needs high quality leadership and an efficient bureaucracy more than new powers.

Any review of the Commission's future role must therefore take into account three elements: its legal responsibilities; the legitimacy and authority of its leadership; and the strength of the administration.

Enforcer of the law

Many of those working inside the Commission seem to believe that unless it is constantly pushing out the boundaries of its legal powers, it will crumble into irrelevance. They see the Commission as the 'lone hero' of European integration. Any other form of co-operation other than the 'Community method' – under which the Commission proposes, the Council and the European Parliament decide, and member-states and the Commission implement – is a betrayal of Europe. This attitude smacks of institutional self-interest. It alienates governments and national parliaments and blinds the Commission to innovative forms of co-operation.

There is a natural division of labour inside the EU. The Commission should take the lead in internal policies, plus other exclusive competences such as trade, which are currently handled in the EU's first pillar. But the Council should be pre-eminent in most external business. The Commission is most effective where it has clearly defined legislative, regulatory and negotiating powers – as in the single market, competition policy, or enlargement. Where its responsibilities are blurred or it has to use other policy tools – as in foreign policy – the Commission's record is far less impressive.

In any case, after enlargement the Commission will face huge challenges in fulfilling its core tasks. It will be much more difficult to devise common solutions to fit a larger, more diverse Union. Even in areas where the Council takes decisions through majority voting, the legislative process is bound to become more tortuous. Implementation, especially in those member-states with weak bureaucracies, will be slow.

The EU has always faced problems in enforcing its rules. Just one member-state, Greece, has ever had to pay a fine for failing to implement and enforce EU laws – and that case took 14 years to wind through the European Court. Other, even more long-standing breaches of EU law go unpunished: France, for instance, has still not implemented a directive protecting wild birds which dates back to the late 1970s.

The Commission needs far more rigorous enforcement procedures. It should set down clear guidelines, including a timetable, for dealing with infringement cases. For instance, the Commission should try to review the member-states' implementation of each new directive after six months, and then launch any infringement procedures that are necessary within a year. The Commission could also ensure that future directives contain non-compliance penalty clauses, so that member-states are forewarned of the costs of non-implementation.

Furthermore, the Commission should propose a treaty amendment that would speed up infringement procedures in the Court of Justice. At present, the Commission needs to win two cases in the European Court before a fine can be imposed on a member-state – an extremely time-consuming procedure. In future, the Commission should only need to win the first judgement to impose a fine. Member-states would still be able to appeal and have the fine repaid. But such a mechanism would greatly reduce member-state foot-dragging in serious cases.

Despite the difficulty of enforcing current rules, the Commission has chosen to focus in its submission to the Convention on a significant extension of its powers. The Commission has a strong case in one area namely JHA. Merging the third pillar – police and judicial co-operation – into the first would extend the Commission's powers in areas such as police co-operation and fighting organised crime. The Community method is appropriate in these areas, since they require legislation at a European level.

However, the Commission also has grand ambitions in the area of foreign policy. The Union's growing efforts to co-ordinate national positions in the Council of Ministers, and to articulate a single voice via Javier Solana, have produced only modest results. The answer, according to the Commission, is for it to assume responsibility for formulating a common foreign and security policy, with the sole right of initiative and a shift to decision-making by qualified majority voting.

Yet the Commission cannot become a kind of European foreign ministry. It lacks the diplomatic experience, has virtually no policy planning expertise and cannot rely on its own intelligence sources or military power. True, the Commission holds many of the instruments of civil power, most obviously in the field of trade and aid policy, and there should be better co-ordination with the EU's broader foreign policy objectives (see Chapter 2). But the most important requirement is for the member-states to first try to reach a solid consensus on their fundamental aims. The public disagreements over policy on Iraq show that EU governments have some way to go.

Could the Community method help to forge such a consensus? On matters of slow, steady diplomacy – such as trade negotiations – it is already quite effective. But in crisis situations that require high diplomacy, and possibly a military response, the Commission would be totally dependent on the member-states, and potentially hostage to their squabbles. Therefore, although the Commission needs to be a strong, authoritative institution, it should focus its efforts on areas of existing EU competence, rather than seek to run foreign policy.

Elect the president

Although the Commission's powers have increased in recent years, for example in areas such as immigration, it is losing credibility with European governments and citizens.

There are several reasons for the Commission's declining status. The launch of monetary union, though successful, has come at a price. Member-states which made huge efforts to qualify for the euro now have little enthusiasm for increasing the EU's powers further. A new generation of European political leaders has emerged, with a greater interest in domestic politics than European integration, and at best an ambivalence about further transfers of power to Brussels.

Increasingly, the Commission's credibility is also suffering from its lack of democratic credentials. The Commission's legitimacy once derived from its supposed independence from national influence, its political impartiality and its ability to define and pursue the common European interest. But the essentially technocratic nature of the Commission's mandate can become a liability when confronted with pressure from democratically elected national governments.

The Commission's legitimacy will be stretched to breaking point in the years ahead. Enlargement will further increase the distance between EU institutions and the man on the street. And the Commission will have a much tougher time trying to enforce the rules across 25 or more countries, which will further undermine its credibility.

The Commission therefore requires some form of democratic mandate, so that it can carry out its core functions effectively. Europe's voters should be given a role in choosing who heads the EU's executive arm. One method would be to allow the pan-European parties to select candidates for the post. In the European elections, voters could cast their votes in the knowledge that the parties favoured one candidate or another. Either the European

Parliament or a broader Congress of MEPs and national MPs could then choose the Commission president.

The election of all the commissioners in this manner could lead to an excessive politicisation of the Commission. But electing only the president would be different. A political mandate for the president would not lead to him or her adopting a party-political agenda in office. Any Commission president would have to strike a cross-party consensus, work with other institutions and keep within the limits of the treaties.

Some critics argue that the election of the president would harm the Commission's regulatory functions, by making it more political. But the Commission is unlike other regulators. For a start, it is a single body regulating a huge range of economic activities. It therefore has an impact on people's daily lives in a way that a normal single industry regulator does not. And unlike the many regulators which monitor businesses in a single sector, the Commission often finds itself policing the activities of elected governments, for example on state aid.

Those who claim that any form of election of the Commission president would fundamentally alter the EU's institutional balance are missing the point. The balance has already shifted to the Commission's detriment. After enlargement, EU decison-making will become a great deal more complicated, and the success of each institution will depend to a far greater degree on the quality of its leadership. The Commission is no exception. It will soon be unable to carry out its duties properly, unless its president is strengthened through a degree of democratic legitimacy.

Running the Commission

An elected Commission president would have more authority over his or her unelected fellow commissioners. There is a desperate need for much greater central co-ordination within the

Commission. Romano Prodi has tried to strengthen its secretariat-general into a department of the president, but there is still a lack of coherence between different parts of the bureaucracy.

The Commission is now more professional in evaluating the resources required to run a particular activity. The Prodi Commission has successfully used an annual resource allocation review to reduce the number of directorates-general (DGs) from 42 to 35. However, there are still far too many different departments and too many staff working in non-priority areas. For instance, DG administration, the Commission's own internal bureaucracy, is still the largest single directorate-general, with a total of 2,500 staff. In contrast, the Justice and Home Affairs department is struggling to meet Council demands for important new legislation with fewer than 200 people.

The Commission should adopt a more radical programme of departmental mergers to increase political control and improve the coherence of its policy-making. For instance, an enterprise directorate-general could oversee all business-related matters, including the internal market, information technology and energy policy, which are at present spread across different directorates-general. The Commission could also free up resources, and make an important gesture to the principle of subsidiarity, by abolishing peripheral directorates-general such as the 600-strong DG for education, culture and sport.

The unwieldy size of the college of commissioners, due to rise to 25 after the coming round of enlargement, also hampers the Commission's internal management. A much smaller group of 12-15 commissioners would improve the collegiality of decision-making, policy co-ordination and the management of the Commission's directorates-general. If the member-states continued to insist on appointing one commissioner each, Prodi's proposal to divide the college into junior commissioners and vice-presidents would be a sensible alternative.

Further changes are also necessary to improve the quality of the bureaucracy. Neil Kinnock, the vice president for reform, has pushed through important reforms that will allow talent to play a bigger role in career development. However, the Commission could do more to raise the overall quality of its staff. The Commission should introduce a code of conduct which clearly sets out the responsibilities and reporting requirements for Commission staff. The existing staff rulebook details pay and conditions rather than internal working practices.

Moreover, the Commission should collaborate more closely with the national bureaucracies. Compulsory exchanges of officials would help the Commission to legislate and regulate with greater sensitivity to the difficulties faced by member-state governments. The Commission would benefit from a much stronger presence of national officials and private sector experts within its ranks. It often lacks the technical expertise and industry experience that are necessary to draft legislation for policy areas such as financial services. Some recently drafted directives, such as that on prospectuses for raising capital on stock markets, have highlighted the Commission's shortcomings in this area. Indeed, it is doubtful whether the Commission should continue with its own corps of specialised civil servants – mostly recruited in their twenties through the *concours* system. The accession of ten new countries, each with staff quotas to be fulfilled, will put the system under great pressure. The Commission would benefit from spreading its net wider and allowing itself to hire more senior people in mid-career.

The Commission also needs to accelerate reforms of its budget management. A new regulation, which comes into force in 2003, will enhance financial control by decentralising responsibility for spending, while introducing more rigorous auditing. But there is still a long way to go in modernising the Commission's systems. One of the Commission's jobs is to oversee the entire EU budget, and a major simplification would help financial control. Why does the EU, unlike most other international organisations, still have the ludicrous distinction between payments and appropriations? Furthermore, the Commission's closing of ranks in response to criticism by Marta Andreasen, its former chief accountant, who was suspended in the summer of 2002 for speaking out, shows that changing the culture of the institution will take many more years.

The need for priorities

The Commission may judge that integration is more or less complete in a whole range of areas, and that it therefore needs to stake out its claim on new territory. But the Commission will find it very hard to carry out its existing functions adequately once enlargement has added a dozen new members to the EU. The Union will become far more complex. The Community method has already reached its limits. New, more flexible forms of integration are needed. But the Commission seems to have little desire to find them. It should be less reluctant to embrace new techniques such as benchmarking, peer-group pressure and exchange of best practice.

The Commission pays lip service to "doing less, but doing it better", in the words of former president Jacques Santer. But it has never asked for a reduction of its responsibilities, so that it can focus on a handful of strategic priorities. The Commission likes to think of itself as the vanguard of European integration. It must ensure that it does not end up fighting a rearguard action in favour of the old ways of doing business.

★

6 Justice and Home Affairs: faster decisions, more secure rights
Heather Grabbe

★ The EU should increase the efficiency of decision-making by using majority voting in more areas, starting with migration and asylum policy, and by making police and judicial co-operation in criminal matters a full competence of the EU's institutions.

★ To increase democratic accountability and legitimacy, the European Parliament should have the power of co-decision in most areas of Justice and Home Affairs, and the European Court of Justice should gain full powers to review legislation concerning internal security.

★ The EU needs to do more to safeguard the rights of individuals affected by cross-border law enforcement. It should set up a Europe-wide legal aid fund, and give the European Ombudsman more power to pursue complaints about the violation of individual rights.

★ To prepare for enlargement, the EU should move ahead with plans for closer co-operation on guarding external borders, both to share the costs more fairly and to ensure uniformly high standards.

The EU is now very active in the field of Justice and Home Affairs (JHA), but it remains a policy area that is little known or understood. JHA now accounts for about 40 per cent of the EU's new legislation. There is strong public support for European countries to work together more closely to deal with common concerns, such as illegal immigration, and threats like international terrorism and transnational crime. EU co-operation in tackling cross-border crime has increased remarkably quickly since September 11th 2001.

JHA co-operation has the potential to make the EU more popular, by showing voters that the Union gives them direct benefits. But if they think that 'Brussels' is responsible for allowing in foreigners and drugs, or for letting their fellow citizens languish in foreign jails on specious charges and without legal services in their own language, they will become more wary of the EU.

There are at least two reasons why the EU needs to make a number of institutional changes at the inter-governmental conference due in 2004. First, decision-making processes in JHA are currently very cumbersome. Second, legislation in the field of Justice and Home Affairs affects the balance of power between governments and citizens, yet democratic oversight of the procedures and decisions taken by justice and interior ministers is sorely lacking. The point of institutional reform should therefore be to increase both the efficiency and the accountability of JHA co-operation, and to add new safeguards for the rights of individuals.

More efficient decision-making

When it started, all the EU's co-operation on JHA was inter-governmental, without the involvement of the Commission, European Parliament or European Court of Justice (ECJ). Therefore when the EU created its three 'pillar' structure within the 1991 Maastricht treaty, JHA was given its own, 'third' pillar (foreign policy made up the second pillar, and traditional Community business the first). At Amsterdam in 1997, the member-states agreed to move most of JHA into the first pillar, but to leave police and judicial co-operation in criminal matters in the third.

What the EU calls Justice and Home Affairs now covers a vast and diverse range of policies. The issues dealt with in the first pillar extend from external borders, to immigration and asylum policy, to judicial co-operation in civil matters. The EU also engages in police and judicial co-operation in criminal matters, but confusingly, these areas are still in the third pillar. The EU thus uses many different decision-making procedures for JHA, which makes deciding on and implementing coherent policies very difficult.

The obvious way to improve this situation would be to merge the third pillar with the first pillar. This would simplify the system, leading to more effective and rapid policy-making, and it would help to increase transparency by making decisions easier to follow. Although there are good reasons to allow national governments a leading role in the EU's foreign and security policy, there is less of a case for a separate structure for JHA. As Chapter 2 makes clear, successful European foreign policies depend on the resources and credibility of member-states, so they cannot be run primarily by EU institutions. But progress in JHA co-operation is mainly about implementing laws, which the first pillar does relatively well.

For example, now that criminals can operate across internal borders unhindered by frontier checks, the EU needs solid cross-border law enforcement and judicial co-operation. However, a merger of the first and third pillars would not automatically mean the 'communitisation' of police and judicial co-operation – that is, putting them fully within the competences of the Commission, the European Parliament and the Court of Justice – as has happened with single market legislation.

There is still a strong inter-governmental element in the JHA policies that are already in the first pillar, including asylum, migration, external border controls and civil law. In these areas, the member-states have limited the role of the European Parliament and the Court of Justice. Moreover, under a transitional period lasting at least until May 2004, the Commission does not have a sole right of initiative, so member-states can put forward their own proposals in these areas. Most important of all, decisions are taken by a unanimous vote, not by a qualified majority.

Therefore a shift of those policy areas which remain in the third pillar to the first would not do much good if decision-making in these areas remained hedged with restrictions on the role of EU institutions. There is not much point in moving the pillars around unless the member-states remove the special procedures that safeguard national interests. At the very least, they should negotiate transitional periods, so that ultimately unanimity remains the rule in only a very few sensitive areas.

The inter-governmental aspects have long snarled up JHA policy-making. If a single member-state holds up progress, only the European Council has a chance of removing the obstacle. For example, the introduction of a common arrest warrant – one of the EU's main responses to the threat of terrorism after September 11th 2001 – was blocked by just one country. Italy's opposition could only be overcome when the prime ministers met in person to thrash out a deal. If the policy had been subject to qualified majority voting (QMV), the other countries could simply have outvoted Italy in the JHA council.

The key to faster decision-making in JHA is to extend QMV to more areas. But no government wants to apply majority voting to everything: each finds one or another issue too sensitive and too close to the heart of national sovereignty. Interestingly, the main objections are not coming from the 'usual suspects'. The traditionally recalcitrant British are pushing for QMV on migration and asylum, whereas the integrationist Germans are very reluctant to see any reduction in their veto rights. The EU should start with QMV on migration and asylum, where the public is demanding urgent and co-ordinated action, and then consider other suitable areas.

Another anomaly is that the Commission and the member-states share the right to initiate legislation on JHA matters, at least until 2004. The Commission has a sole right of initiative on other first pillar issues. Member-states are certainly capable of making well-prepared and timely proposals on JHA, and the Commission often suffers from overload, so this joint right of initiative has been useful in the pioneering years of JHA policy. But member-state initiatives have sometimes overlapped with or prevented discussion of Commission proposals. On the whole, the Council should set the overall direction and aims of JHA policy, and then leave the Commission to work out which measures are necessary, as happens in other areas of EU policy. In the longer run, it would be more efficient for one body to implement the Council's strategy, which means giving the Commission the sole right to initiate legislation.

Finally, the EU should simplify the confusing range of different legal instruments that it uses for JHA at European level. It has so far used special instruments such as 'framework decisions' that make JHA harder to understand. The EU should work towards using the same legal instruments that are used in the rest of the first pillar, namely directives and regulations. Then the EU's legislative system would be less complicated and more transparent.

Single market methods for justice

One of the EU's greatest successes has been the single market project, steadily implemented since the 1980s. To advance JHA co-operation, the Union needs to use some of the same methods. A central principle of the single market is 'mutual recognition', which allows national authorities to recognise the work done and decisions taken by their counterparts in other member-states as valid in their own countries. This method obviates the need for extensive harmonisation of national systems of regulation. Another ingredient of the success of the single market was the widespread introduction of qualified majority voting.

The application of mutual recognition to JHA, together with an extension of QMV, would help to ensure that national systems could work together efficiently. There is little point in ministers agreeing to share information and work together if judges, police officers and officials do not want to collaborate with their counterparts in other EU countries. So far, practitioners have been very reluctant to recognise other members' systems of justice and law enforcement as equivalent to their own. Another problem is that the various governments' IT systems and administrative frameworks are often incompatible. Ministers have tried to promote greater compatibility by using the 'open method of co-ordination' – that is, agreements on common targets, benchmarking and peer-group pressure. However, the open method is not enough on its own, and governments will also need to step up their use of traditional, harder methods of decision-making.

One difference between JHA and the single market is that it is not feasible for the member-states to harmonise national legal systems in the way that they harmonised business regulations. Any attempt to change one part of a national legal system is liable to have knock-on effects on other areas. The 15 member-states have very different legal systems, and the accession of new members will bring further diversity. No country wants to give up its legal tradition in favour of another, which means that only a limited harmonisation of procedures is feasible. But they can and should start to recognise one another's judicial decisions.

Protecting freedoms

The EU responded quickly to the terrorist attacks of September 11th with new measures to track down and apprehend suspected terrorists. The most important of these were a common definition of terrorism, a common list of suspected terrorist organisations, and the December 2001 agreement on an EU-wide search and arrest warrant. Citizens will not accept free movement across the borders of the EU-25 if they fear that criminals and terrorists can easily take refuge in another member-state. The common arrest warrant should thus be implemented as quickly as possible. But it needs to be accompanied by measures to ensure that standards of law enforcement and the protection of citizens' rights are maintained at high levels across the EU.

Unfortunately, the recent moves to extend EU involvement in JHA have not been balanced by efforts to enhance the rights of citizens affected by EU policies and their implementation. So far, the public has been generally supportive of tighter European co-operation on security and crime, recognising that countries have to work together. But if the result turns out to be an erosion of individual liberties, the EU could become even more unpopular than it is already.

Oversight of the emerging European judicial system is woefully inadequate. Because JHA ministers take many decisions behind closed doors, only national governments can monitor EU activities that may impinge on individual freedoms, and their monitoring is often poor. The EU has given Europol, its police liaison office, a new counter-terrorism mandate, including the exchange of information with the US authorities. This is a welcome step, but the activities of Europol and Eurojust – the EU's embryonic prosecutions agency – must be subject to independent oversight. National police forces are accountable to the courts, while the courts themselves operate within constitutional frameworks and are subject to parliamentary scrutiny. At European level too, the actions of the executive should be subject to the control of the other branches of government – the parliament and judiciary. For this reason, the European Parliament should have an extensive right of scrutiny over JHA, including the right of co-decision with the Council in all but the most sensitive areas, like intelligence-sharing.

JHA decisions should also come under the full jurisdiction of the European Court of Justice. At the moment, the Court has only a limited mandate in JHA, so it has little scope to review legislation in this area. It has no jurisdiction to review whether Europol has exceeded its powers, or whether national enforcement agencies have stepped beyond their mandate in EU-approved operations. Nor can the ECJ force member-states to live up to their promises. If the Court had full jurisdiction over JHA, a member-state that dragged its feet over implementing EU legislation – as Italy is currently doing with the common arrest warrant – could face infringement proceedings. An extension of the Court's remit would also help to protect individuals who may be affected by JHA measures. For example, the Court could assess whether a new measure was compatible with the EU's treaties and its Charter of Fundamental Rights. The EU should also increase the Court's budget to ensure that it can cope with the rising case-load.

The EU's decisions on matters of internal security have a direct impact not only on companies and governments but also on the rights of individuals across Europe. At present, an individual may complain about the violation of his or her rights by another member-state or an EU institution through a national legal system, but this is a long and cumbersome procedure. The EU therefore needs to put in place additional safeguards at the EU level.

The new EU arrest warrant will allow judges and police forces to extradite suspects automatically. But to ensure that they are treated fairly, suspects need to have their rights to a fair trial strengthened. The EU should ensure that anyone sent for trial in another EU country has access to a competent lawyer and to an interpreter, so that he or she can follow court proceedings. All the member-states should set up a central fund for legal aid, as well as citizens' advice bureaux that can deal with cross-border cases. The EU also needs to create a 'Eurobail' system so that indicted suspects can stay in custody in their home country while waiting for their case to come to trial, instead of being held for a long period in a foreign gaol.

Data protection is a sensitive issue for EU citizens. The EU has set up a number of vast databases – such as the Schengen Information System (SIS) and the Europol databases – that contain information on EU and non-EU citizens alike. These databases are vital tools for fighting crime and terrorism. But the EU should ensure uniform protection of all data, in accordance with the right to privacy articles of the European Convention on Human Rights, and the associated case law. Individuals can gain access to their SIS files only through national data protection laws, which differ between countries. In addition, it is difficult for a citizen to seek to amend incorrect information on his or her record. Given that the databases are held centrally, there should be an EU-wide mechanism for amendment through a central access-point.

The EU needs to develop a more coherent framework for the protection of fundamental rights. There is currently a confusion of overlapping sources of authority. The EU treaties refer to the protection of fundamental rights in several places, without listing the rights themselves. In addition, all the member-states are signatories of the European Convention on Human Rights, which is an international convention outside the EU framework. At the Nice summit in December 2000 the EU's governments declared their support for the Charter of Fundamental Rights, but it remains a declaratory document without any direct legal force. It should be incorporated into the EU's treaties, a move which most member-states favour. Furthermore, the EU should incorporate the European Convention on Human Rights into Community law. Then lawyers and judges could use the well-established case-law that is associated with the Convention to interpret the rights of individuals. In addition, the European Court of Justice should gain the power to annul measures that do not respect fundamental rights.

Individuals can already complain to the European Ombudsman if they suffer from maladministration on the part of the EU's institutions. However, few citizens know about the Ombudsman's existence, perhaps because he cannot propose changes to EU laws that affect fundamental rights. A first step would be for the Ombudsman to gain the power to request an opinion from the ECJ. In the longer term, he should also be able to bring cases to the Court. The remedies available to individuals for protecting their rights should be made much clearer in the treaties, and widely advertised throughout the Union.

Policing Europe's frontiers

The Seville European Council decided in June 2002 on further steps to strengthen external border protection. In addition to introducing measures to combat illegal immigration and making a further push towards a common policy on asylum, the EU's leaders endorsed a study from the Italian government on the feasibility of a European border police force. Under current plans, the EU has no intention of creating a whole new force to rival existing national border guards. But by the end of 2002, the member-states' national forces are supposed to be able to carry out joint operations at external borders. Now that the EU's external borders are effectively common to all member-states, the EU must work rapidly towards a consistently high standard of protection along the entire frontier.

The creation of a common strategy for managing external borders would be a welcome step to protect the Union's residents from cross-border crime, terrorism and other threats. Since travel in the Schengen area is free of passport checks, every country has an interest in the good management of its neighbours' borders. The costs of policing the border should thus be borne by all the member-states and not just those on the front line. In addition, after enlargement, many of the front-line member-states will be poorer countries which will need help to meet the expense of tighter Schengen controls. But in defending its external borders more rigorously, the EU must make sure it does not cut off the countries that remain outside. The new controls must be balanced with measures to facilitate legitimate travel for business-people and tourists.

★

7 The European Parliament's path to maturity
Alasdair Murray

★ In the last ten years, the European Parliament has developed into an effective scrutiny body. However, it is not yet able to review properly every area of EU policy-making. Co-decision procedures should apply to all legislation that is subject to qualified majority voting, while Parliament should gain the power to suggest amendments to, or reject, all elements of the EU budget.

★ Parliament should be able to issue 'subpoenas', to force key witnesses to appear before its investigative committees.

★ The MEPs should be able to initiate a couple of pieces of legislation each year, although the Council would be able to veto such laws.

★ The Parliament should have the right to set its own pay rates and to choose where it sits.

The European Parliament's decision in July 2001 to reject the takeover directive provided hard proof of the institution's increasingly powerful role on the European stage. The Parliament's influence has risen dramatically in the decade since the Maastricht treaty introduced co-decision procedures, which placed Parliament on an equal footing with the Council of Ministers for many legislative matters.

The Parliament has proven its worth by examining, amending and sometimes rejecting European legislation, monitoring the budget and scrutinising Commission actions. MEPs now work in tandem with the Council to amend and pass EU legislation on issues as diverse as accountancy standards and waste disposal rules. The Parliament can veto legislation – as happened in the case of the takeover directive – if MEPs are unable to reach agreement with the Council on the content of a new directive. And the Parliament has shown that it can use its powers of investigation to crack down on European Commission fraud and mismanagement – as it did when it threatened a vote of no confidence to force the resignation of the Santer Commission in 1999.

Indeed, MEPs arguably enjoy more power and independence than many of their national counterparts, who work in parliaments dominated by the governing executive. The Parliament is also the most open of the EU's institutions, a fact not lost on the hundreds of lobbyists who throng its buildings in Brussels and Strasbourg. Businesses, pressure groups and even a few private citizens understand that MEPs are far more likely to take up a grievance than member-state governments or Commission officials – and that the Parliament now has the power to make significant changes to legislation.

Yet the European Parliament remains the least visible of the three main EU institutions, despite its increased powers and direct democratic mandate. In part, this reflects a public perception of the Parliament which has not yet caught up with the reality of its new powers. Voter turnout has fallen at every European poll since direct elections were introduced in 1979. The European media, in particular, find the Parliament difficult to cover properly, as MEPs endlessly commute between Brussels and Strasbourg. The press find it far easier to write articles about the set-piece battles of the Council than the detailed amendments that are debated in European Parliament committees.

Moreover, the Parliament cannot yet oversee all areas of EU policy-making. In institutional terms, the European Parliament is in late adolescence. It enjoys a great deal of grown-up power and independence through its role in amending and passing legislation and parts of the EU's budget. However, MEPs lack powers of amendment or veto in some areas of legislation, such as agriculture, and in Justice and Home Affairs. And although MEPs can sack the Commission, they cannot decide their own salaries or even where they meet.

There is a strong case for strengthening the European Parliament by giving MEPs a role in the election of the Commission president, if not to grant them the sole right of appointment. However, the Convention on the future of Europe should not ignore a number of other reforms which would increase the Parliament's external visibility and enhance its scrutiny role. The Parliament's co-decision and budgetary powers should be extended into those policy areas, such as agriculture, which remain the prerogative of the Council. The Convention should also consider innovations, such as a limited right of legislative initiative and the power to subpoena witnesses for inquiries. Above all, however, MEPs should be able to set their own pay and chose their own meeting place.

Elect the Commission president

The direct involvement of MEPs in the selection of the Commission president would strengthen the Commission's accountability to the Parliament, and make the appointment process much more transparent. Chapter 5 describes how the principal political groupings could fight the European elections, each proposing a candidate for the Commission presidency. Such a system should aid the development of truly pan-European political parties: in future the European political groupings would need to agree not only on a candidate for president but also on a more coherent common manifesto.

A Congress, consisting of equal numbers of MEPs and national parliamentarians, would meet shortly after the European Parliament elections to choose the new president. The president would thus enjoy two sources of legitimacy. The Congress could also meet once a year to listen to and vote on the Commission president's annual work programme, as the US Congress does for the American president's 'State of the Union' address. But only the European Parliament would continue to monitor the Commission's work on a day-to-day basis.

The direct involvement of national MPs would have one important benefit: it would ensure that the new president had genuine Europe-wide electoral appeal and was not simply a European Parliament party hack. The Council should retain the right to veto the appointment of the president on a unanimous basis, although it would be politically difficult to ever use this power. Moreover, the Council should continue to appoint the other commissioners – which will ensure a diversity of both nationality and political background. Each national parliament should have the opportunity to ratify the commissioner nominated by his or her government.

The EU should also undertake one further reform to increase the involvement of national parliaments in EU affairs. At present, MPs are able to meet and exchange views on European issues at COSAC – the conference of Community and European affairs committees. However, COSAC remains an obscure body that cannot attract senior national parliamentarians, because it has no power. The EU should beef up COSAC and give it the power to ask the European Court of Justice to rule on whether a new law violated the principle of subsidiarity. This revamped committee should also conduct an annual review of existing EU legislation and propose a list of outmoded laws to be removed from the EU's rulebook. The heads of government would then take a political decision on which of them should be repealed, and instruct the EU institutions to implement that decison. Such a procedure would help ensure that national parliaments maintained a stake in the EU's political system.

More powers on legislation and the budget

The European Parliament has significant legislative powers in the form of the co-decision procedure. The Parliament can also amend and veto the annual EU budget, although it has not used the veto power since 1984. Instead, the Parliament now works with the Council and Commission to devise multi-annual 'financial perspectives' which fix the overall size of the EU budget for a defined period – the present seven year agreement lasts until 2006. But the Parliament does use its powers of amendment to modify individual items of expenditure, such as spending on structural funds or training, when it reviews the EU's annual budget each autumn. Nevertheless, any amendments must respect the overall budget lines agreed under the financial perspective.

However, some key legislative and budgetary policies remain beyond the Parliament's control – most notably in the areas of agricultural policy, Justice and Home Affairs, and taxation. In the past, the Council has justified these legislative exemptions on the basis that they were so sensitive that they should be the preserve of member-state governments and national parliaments. However, this argument makes little sense when member-states have agreed to take decisions by qualified majority, as is the case with agricultural policy. The Nice treaty would increase the number of policy areas where the Council can legislate using qualified majority voting (QMV) without co-decision procedures – most notably in the realm of a common asylum policy.

Indeed, there is a real danger that crucial legislation, especially in the sensitive area of Justice and Home Affairs, will receive only cursory parliamentary scrutiny unless the European Parliament gains the power of co-decision. National parliaments examine legislation after it has been agreed at a European level and can only influence the way legislation is implemented at the member-state level – they cannot amend an EU directive itself. Moreover, a national parliament cannot hold a government to account and take up legitimate concerns about the quality of a new EU law, if that member-state has already voted against the legislation but lost under QMV.

This makes it essential for MEPs to examine EU laws, to scrutinise their effectiveness and to express the concerns of governments and national parliaments which may oppose parts of a directive. Otherwise it is possible that far-reaching legislation on Justice and Home Affairs – such as an EU-wide crackdown on illegal migration – could be agreed at the European level with no proper parliamentary review. A simple rule of thumb should be that all measures decided by the Council using QMV should also be subject to co-decision. Thus co-decision should be introduced to all Justice and Home Affairs legislative issues, which are likely to be decided on a QMV basis after 2004, and to agriculture, but not to taxation, which will remain subject to unanimity.

The Parliament is also excluded from amending the part of the EU's budget defined as 'compulsory expenditure' – in practice, the 45 per cent that is spent on agriculture. The division of the EU budget into compulsory and non-compulsory expenditure lines is arbitrary and a matter of frequent dispute between the Parliament and the Council. The effect is to ring-fence the vast majority of payments under the Common Agricultural Policy from effective parliamentary scrutiny. The Parliament is able to propose modifications to how this part of the budget is spent, but the Council retains the final say on where the money goes.

There is no logical justification for this exclusion. It remains in place simply because some member-states, most notably Britain, fear that the Parliament would come under pressure from the vocal rural lobby and try to increase payments to farmers. Other member-states, such as France, fear that a reformist majority in the Parliament might try and cut payments.

It is absurd that the Parliament can amend the remainder of the budget, on which it has the power of veto, but that it has no direct powers over agricultural payments. It should gain the power to amend any item of expenditure within the EU budget. This modest reform would not restrict the Council's right to control the ultimate size of the EU budget, the principal categories under which the money is spent, or the means by which budget revenue is raised. However, it would enable the Parliament to fulfil more effectively its job of monitoring the EU's budget. A single budgetary procedure would also help to make the EU's complex finances more transparent to the European public.

Increase Parliament's powers of scrutiny

The European Parliament employs its committee structure in an increasingly effective manner to scrutinise the non-legislative elements of EU policy-making. The economic and monetary affairs committee, for instance, holds a quarterly hearing with the president of the European Central Bank – although the Parliament has no direct powers over monetary policy. The Parliament is also able to establish ad hoc committees of inquiry to investigate breaches of Community law or Commission mismanagement. In recent years, the Parliament has conducted high-profile investigations into the 'mad cow' crisis and the Echelon intelligence system.

However, in some key areas, such as foreign and security policy, the Parliament only has very limited powers of oversight. Few MEPs expect to play a direct role in sensitive foreign policy matters – national parliaments also lack the power to control their governments in this area. At the European level, it is the Council, rather than the Commission, which takes the lead on foreign policy, the Parliament has no formal powers to amend or veto foreign policy decisions.

MEPs arguably waste far too much time passing meaningless resolutions on foreign policy issues over which they have no direct powers. But the European Parliament should be able to oversee EU foreign policy decisions, just as national parliaments do for national decisions. In particular, the Parliament should be able to quiz key officials on a regular basis. Javier Solana, the High Representative for the Common Foreign and Security Policy, is often reluctant to attend parliamentary sessions, in part due to his heavy travel schedule, but also because he believes that he is accountable to the Council alone. The Council should confirm that the Parliament has the right to summon and question key officials working on foreign policy issues, including Solana.

The EU institutions are working together to solve the specific problem of how the Parliament can be kept informed of sensitive security matters. In line with practice in most member-states, the Council will need to establish a vetting procedure for members of the committee which covers the foreign and defence policy, and some sessions will need to take place behind closed doors.

The Parliament also needs greater powers of scrutiny over the Commission's implementing powers. The Commission is able to produce a wide array of detailed measures – covering everything from health and safety rules to securities market regulation – without having to go through full co-decision procedures. Instead, the Commission works with small committees, consisting of expert member-state representatives, to devise implementing measures – a system dubbed 'comitology' in EU jargon. Most comitology measures are highly technical and not politically controversial. However, these committees sometimes take contentious decisions – such as the lifting of the ban on British beef exports.

Unlike the Council, the Parliament has no formal right to block or amend decisions taken by comitology procedures. However, the recent agreement between the Commission, Council and Parliament on the Lamfalussy group recommendations for EU financial services legislation could provide a way forward. The Lamfalussy group called for the establishment of two new comitology committees to write the detailed rules for the EU's programme to create a single market in securities. The Parliament has now gained the power to recommend changes during a three-month scrutiny period. The Parliament has also won a 'sunset' clause, meaning that the Commission's powers to implement these committees' decisions will expire or have to be renewed after four years. The EU should extend the Lamfalussy model to all implementing measures adopted through the comitology system.

Finally, the European Parliament's powers of inquiry need strengthening. At present, the Parliament's right to conduct a committee of inquiry and call officials is governed by a non-binding inter-institutional agreement. The vast majority of EU and national officials and politicians voluntarily attend parliamentary hearings. However, Douglas Hogg, the former British agriculture minister, refused a European Parliament request to attend a hearing on BSE. Moreover, if Europe suffered an Enron-style corporate collapse, the Parliament would have no power to force key executives, auditors or expert witnesses to appear before a committee of inquiry. Some MEPs complain that the lack of a formal power of compulsion means that even when witnesses do attend hearings, they do not feel obliged to tell the truth.

The Parliament should gain the power to 'subpoena' key witnesses for its inquiries – subject to two safeguards. The specific committee of inquiry should be able to request the subpoena, but a majority vote in the full chamber would have to activate this power. And the Council, acting by unanimity, should be able to veto a subpoena request in exceptional cases. The subpoena power, which is familiar to many in the context of the US Congress, would also raise the Parliament's profile in the European media and with the EU population in general.

A private member's right of initiative

The fact that the European Parliament, unlike most national parliaments, lacks a right of legislative initiative is one reason why EU electorates perceive it as a weak institution. In reality, the gap between the European and national parliaments' legislative powers is not so great. In most member-states, the executive preserves a near monopoly on the right of initiative. Most national parliamentarians carry out a similar role to their European colleagues, scrutinising and amending legislation prepared by the government. Moreover, the European Parliament can request that the Commission prepares a specific item of legislation – as it did for a recent directive clarifying the rules for cross-border car insurance.

Such constitutional subtleties are largely lost on European electors. However, a reform which granted individual MEPs a limited right of initiative would increase Parliament's visibility across the EU. MEPs could include any plans for new laws in their election addresses, thereby gaining greater media exposure.

At the beginning of each year, any MEP that had won the support of 50 colleagues could bid to win parliamentary time for a new legislative proposal. MEPs would then choose two pieces of proposed legislation, either through a ballot or a lottery system. The legislation would proceed through the co-decision procedure, leaving the Council with the power of veto by QMV. However, the Commission would also give its opinion on whether the new legislation was compatible both with existing EU law and the principle of subsidiarity.

The main objection to such a reform – heard even among some MEPs – is that it would upset the balance of power between the EU's institutions. In particular, if the Parliament won the power to initiate legislation, the Commission would lose the sole right of initiative and that could encourage the Council to seek similar powers. However, the Council already possesses its own right of initiative, in areas such as foreign policy and Justice and Home Affairs. Moreover, the Parliament would only be able to pursue two bills each year, some of which would fail at Council level. Indeed, the reform would be largely symbolic: the Commission would continue to run the main legislative agenda and the Parliament's chief role would remain that of amending and scrutinising Commission-led legislation. However, a private member's right of initiative would enable the Parliament to plug any gaps in the EU's legislative agenda. Equally important, it would ensure that the European Parliament played a role more akin to that of member-state parliaments. And that, in turn, should improve the Parliament's visibility with the European electorate.

A permanent seat

MEPs are frequently condemned for their lavish pay and perks, and for wasting vast amounts of taxpayer money maintaining buildings in both Brussels and Strasbourg. Yet the European Parliament does not have the power to set pay for MEPs or to choose where it sits.

Member-state governments pick up the bill for MEP salaries, paying the same rate as national parliamentarians. As a result, there is a huge discrepancy in pay rates: German MEPs earn roughly three times as much as their Portuguese colleagues. These discrepancies mean that many MEPs use travel expenses, which are in the Parliament's control, to supplement their salaries – Brussels is, after all, a considerably more expensive city than Lisbon.

Moreover, it is the member-states which insist that MEPs persist with the hugely expensive and disruptive practice of holding a monthly session in Strasbourg. The European Parliament spends €169 million a year travelling back and forth to Strasbourg – a figure that is expected to rise to €200 million following enlargement. EU governments confirmed in the Amsterdam treaty of 1997 that the Parliament's formal seat would continue to be Strasbourg, while Brussels was reserved for 'additional plenary sessions and committee meetings'. In turn, the Parliament's general secretariat is supposed to be based in Luxembourg, 200 kilometres from Brussels, although some key officials have their offices in Brussels.

The vast majority of MEPs want to dispense with Strasbourg and move the Parliament's staff out of Luxembourg. Apart from the issue of time and cost, Strasbourg is far removed from the other institutions and key officials. While commissioners reluctantly make the trip to Eastern France, representatives of the EU presidency rarely find the time to attend Strasbourg sessions. The Parliament simply cannot do its job properly in Strasbourg.

It is time that member-states amended the treaty to allow the Parliament to take full control of its internal affairs on issues such as pay and location. Such a reform would confirm that the Parliament had at last reached maturity.

★

8 The European Central Bank: the case for reform
Katinka Barysch

★ The Convention on the future of Europe should put ECB reform high on its agenda. To enshrine the ECB's role and purpose in a future EU constitution would strengthen its legitimacy.

★ EU enlargement will require a streamlining of the ECB's Governing Council. National central bank governors should be represented through a system of rotation, with permanent seats reserved only for the largest member-states and the Executive Board.

★ The ECB itself can do much to become more accountable. It should re-define its policy targets and improve its communication strategies. It should be required to write an open letter to the European Parliament and the Euro Group if it misses its inflation targets.

The European Central Bank (ECB) has so far received little attention in the debate about the future of Europe. This is surprising. Not only does the ECB play a pivotal role in Europe's project of economic integration, it is also one of the few EU institutions with real supranational powers. If the ECB fails to elicit the trust and approval of European citizens, what chance is there for further integration, either economic or political?

Although the euro has proved a success and eurozone inflation is low, the ECB is often seen as arrogant and aloof. Unlike the Bank of England, it refuses to publish details of its policy meetings. Unlike the US Federal Reserve, it lacks – at least for now – a strong and charismatic leader. How can the EU become legitimate, even loved, if its key economic policy institution appears to be an impenetrable fortress?

The ECB is quite possibly the most independent central bank in the world. Its defences against any form of political meddling are even stronger than those of the famously autonomous German Bundesbank. There are sound economic reasons for this, which are widely accepted by economists and politicians alike. Nevertheless, the ECB can and should do more to strike a better balance between splendid isolation and democratic accountability.

Gridlock after enlargement?

Existing proposals for ECB reform largely concentrate on questions of transparency and accountability. But these may be missing a key point as they ignore the impact of EU enlargement on ECB decision-making. The ECB's key task, as far as most European citizens are concerned, is to contribute to the health of the European economy. The ECB cannot force European governments to reform their sclerotic labour markets. It cannot directly influence fiscal policy. But it can and must ensure that monetary policy provides a framework for sustained and balanced growth in the entire euro area.

For this, the ECB needs to be able to react swiftly and decisively when growth slumps or price rises threaten to get out of control. However, it is exactly this ability that may be under threat. Another ten countries will join the EU as early as 2004. Most are keen to adopt the euro as soon as possible. If the current outs – Denmark, Sweden and the UK– also decide to join, the number of countries in the eurozone may well double before the end of the decade. The ECB's main policy-making body, the Governing

Council, would then grow from an already unwieldy 18 members to 30 or more. The Executive Board – which consists of the ECB president, the vice president, and four other appointed officials – would find itself in a hopeless minority vis-à-vis 22 to 25 national central bank governors.

Officially, the Governing Council sets eurozone interest rates through majority voting, but many ECB watchers are convinced that it seeks a consensus. After enlargement, this will hardly be an option since a body with 30-odd members would be prone to gridlock. Voting, however, would also become much more complicated. Not only will there be many more members, they will also be more economically diverse.

After enlargement, small and fast-growing countries will dominate in the ECB Council. Unlike in other EU bodies, votes in the ECB are not weighted. Estonia, with 1.4 million inhabitants and a GDP of less than €10 billion, will have the same voting power as Germany, with 82 million citizens and an economy of more than €2,000 billion. This matters because national central bank governors will base their monetary policy preferences at least partly on conditions in their own countries rather than in the eurozone as a whole.

Although it is unlikely that the new members will move through the business cycle in unison, they share certain structural characteristics that set them apart from the larger and more mature EU member-states. With an average per capita GDP of less than 40 per cent of the EU average, the Eastern European applicants have ample scope for catch-up. This implies that both their growth and inflation rates will – and should – be higher than those of the existing member-states for many years to come. The new members may therefore want higher interest rates than the EU's 'core' economies. Together with other fast-growing countries, such as Greece, Ireland and Portugal, they would easily gain the majority necessary to make their views prevail.

An enlarged Governing Council could thus set a monetary policy that stifles growth in Europe's largest economies – a truly unsavoury thought, given that Germany, France, Italy and the UK (which may have joined by then) would together account for more than two-thirds of the enlarged eurozone's GDP. Questions of transparency and accountability aside, a paralysed or deeply divided ECB would appear neither credible nor particularly legitimate in the eyes of the European public.

Governors will have to take a back seat

EU governments should therefore make a priority of reforming ECB decision-making. The EU's Nice summit in December 2000 called on the ECB and the Commission to produce reform proposals. In 2002, the ECB was still mulling over whether reform was necessary at all. The Bank has said it wants to see if the Nice treaty (which contains the reform mandate) is ratified by the Irish.

The reform of the ECB is such an important subject that it needs serious reflection rather than behind-the-scenes deal-making. The EU should place ECB reform firmly on the agenda of the Convention and the 2004 inter-governmental conference. The smaller countries will resist any changes in ECB voting rules. But it may be easier for the large countries to push the small ones into a bargain that links ECB reform to other issues in the Convention before the new members have occupied their seats in Frankfurt.

Any durable reform will have to limit the size of the Governing Council. A system of rotation would allow the EU to cap the number of national central bank governors with voting rights at the current 12. Each governor would serve a three or four year term, according to a pre-agreed schedule. However, this would still leave the Governing Council heavily dominated by small countries, while the central bankers from larger countries waited impatiently for their turn. It would be better to let the large member-states keep a permanent seat, just like the Federal Reserve Bank of New York has a permanent seat in the US Federal Reserve policy-making body. This would make political sense, since French or German resistance to leaving monetary policy to their smaller neighbours could frustrate all attempts at ECB reform. It would also make economic sense since the ECB Governing Council should include representatives with an in-depth knowledge of the EU's largest economies. If the large countries were to retain permanent seats for their national central bank governors, they should stop insisting that they are also represented on the ECB Executive Board. This would keep the door open for an ECB president and/or vice president from one of the smaller countries.

And now for transparency

If a rotation system were adopted, ECB decision-making could become more heavily dominated by the technocrats of the Executive Board. This may be good for efficiency, but it would throw the ECB's lack of democratic accountability into even sharper relief. Further efforts to make ECB decision-making more legitimate in the eyes of the European public should therefore accompany any institutional reform. The ECB cannot and should not be made subject to direct political control. But it could move towards greater accountability by setting out clear targets and explaining better why it has or has not met them.

The ECB has already taken a couple of steps towards greater transparency, such as reporting to the European Parliament four times a year, instead of just once as required by the Maastricht treaty. But its communication with policy-makers, markets and the public at large has remained clumsy. The ECB president does talk to the media immediately after the first policy meeting of each month. But he only explains why the ECB has or has not cut interest rates, without shedding much light on the preceding debate and the strength of dissenting opinions.

One thing the ECB could do to improve its image would be to publish the minutes of its policy meetings within a reasonable timeframe (it grudgingly agrees to make them public after a 16-year wait, which is not good enough). The ECB may well be right to argue that revealing the voting records of individual governors would be inappropriate in the European context, not only because of the current tendency towards consensus, but also because it would open the door to political pressure. Little speaks against the publication of anonymous minutes, however. These would probably reveal that – contrary to its rather dogmatic image – the ECB does indeed care about growth and employment.

A clear yardstick for performance

For now, however, the publication of minutes may not help ECB accountability very much, since the targets against which the Bank's performance is measured are rather obscure. The Maastricht treaty requires the ECB to aim at 'price stability' in the eurozone, but leaves the Bank free to determine what this means and how to achieve it. The Bank has decided to base its monetary policy on two 'pillars'. It keeps one eye on the growth of money supply (M3) and another on other factors influencing consumer price inflation. It does not set official targets for either, relying on medium-term 'reference values' instead.

But although both M3 growth and inflation have stubbornly refused to stay close to their reference values (4.5 and 2 per cent or below, respectively), the ECB has cut or raised interest rates in defiance of what the money and inflation data would have suggested. If the central bank is free to ignore its own policy targets, what hope is there for outside observers to measure its performance?

A more realistic and workable monetary policy framework is needed. But so far the ECB has persistently ignored calls from economists and policy-makers to dismantle the obviously useless money supply pillar, and to redefine its inflation target. Not only is the inflation target too low – in 2002, the ECB was on course to miss it for the third year running out of four – but it is also lop-sided: it only requires inflation to be lower than 2 per cent, but does not categorically rule out zero inflation or falling prices, both of which can be very harmful to economic growth. The ECB should contemplate adopting an inflation objective that is both higher and symmetrical, which means that inflation should not be allowed to fall below a certain threshold.

Some have suggested that a political body, such as the European Parliament or the Euro Group (the finance ministers of the eurozone countries), should define the ECB's target of price stability.[7] This may be too bold a step, at a time when the ECB is still struggling to establish its reputation for independence with international markets. For now, let the ECB continue to set its own targets, but hold it publicly accountable if it does not meet them. Just as the Bank of England has to explain itself to the UK Treasury, the ECB should be required to write an open letter to both the chair of the Euro Group and the president of the European Parliament every time inflation remains above or below the reference value for, say, three months in row. Publicity is a potent disciplinary tool in the EU – as shown by the outcry that follows each time the EU reproaches a country for endangering the fiscal targets of the Stability and Growth Pact. Open letters from the ECB could help to trigger a Europe-wide discussion of its performance, which would be a major step towards greater accountability.

[7] 'How to reform the European Central Bank', J-P Fitoussi and Jérôme Creel, CER October 2002.

Monetary policy is not a simply a technical issue. It is an acutely political process, especially in the EU, where fiscal constraints (such as the Stability and Growth Pact) and the on-going deregulation of labour and product markets leave national governments with less scope to steer their own economies. To take account of the political nature of monetary policy, the Convention should include the role and purpose of the ECB in any future European constitution.

★